IS IT TRUE WHAT THEY
SAY ABOUT SHAKESPEARE?

IS IT TRUE WHAT THEY SAY ABOUT

SHAKESPEARE?

❀

STANLEY WELLS

LONG BARN BOOKS

Published by
LONG BARN BOOKS
Ebrington, Gloucestershire GL55 6NW

Copyright © Stanley Wells
Illustrations copyright © Shakespeare Birthplace Trust (pp. 13, 77, 78, and
163);
Illustrations copyright © Bridgeman Art Library (p. 57)
Illustrations copyright © National Portrait Gallery, London (p. 79)

Printed and Bound by Compass Press Ltd

ISBN 13: 978-1-902421-23-0

To Poppy and Eric Anderson

Contents

❀

❖

Is it true that this is a genuine portrait of Shakespeare?

VERDICT

See p. 106

PREFACE

❖

In this little book I examine some of the principal current beliefs, myths and legends associated with the name of William Shakespeare in the attempt to distinguish between fact, reasonable conjecture, speculation, and pure fiction. I also include a short life of Shakespeare in which I bring together in a consecutive narrative the principal facts relating to his life. This is a personal book in the sense that I do not disguise my own views, though at the same time I attempt to present the evidence fairly.

I draw extensively on my own work over many years, but must express an especial obligation to books by my late friend S. Schoenbaum, especially to his wonderfully comprehensive and witty study of Shakespearian biography, *Shakespeare's Lives* (1988, revised 1991). I have not thought it necessary in a book of this nature to give chapter and verse for all my references, but the notes on p. 175 provide some that may be useful. Quotations from early writings are in modern spelling except where the original is relevant. At the back of this book you will find some suggestions for other books that you may like to read.

Picture Acknowledgements:

p. 13, 77, 78 and 163 Shakespeare Birthplace Trust

p. 57, Bridgeman Art Library

p. 79, National Portrait Gallery, London

PART ONE:

THE LIFE

Is it true that...?

HE WAS BORN IN
SHAKESPEARE'S BIRTHPLACE

WHAT IS THE EVIDENCE?

Shakespeare's father, John, was fined in 1552 for creating a muck hill, or dung heap, in Henley Street, Stratford-upon-Avon. This was probably in front of the house now known as Shakespeare's Birthplace, part of which he bought in 1556, eight years before William's birth. It seems likely that he was living in this house in 1564. In 1575 he bought additional property, probably the other part of the Birthplace, the whole of which he is known to have owned by 1590. It formed a substantial property, with extensive grounds. Though he could have been born somewhere else – his grandmother's house, perhaps, or a friend's, or even a ditch – it is natural enough to suppose that William was born in the house that his parents owned and lived in, and an upstairs room is traditionally identified as the birth room.

VERDICT

Probably true

HE WAS BORN ON
ST GEORGE'S DAY, 23 APRIL

WHAT IS THE EVIDENCE?

The parish register of Stratford-upon-Avon records his baptism on Wednesday 26 April 1564. The bust in Holy Trinity Church says that he died on 23 April 1616 at the age of 53. If he was 53 by that day, he must have been born on or before 23 April. In that age of high infant mortality it was usual for babies to be baptized within a day or two of their birth, so it's perfectly possible that William was born on 23 April, which by long tradition is celebrated as his birthday. The essayist Thomas de Quincey (1785-1859) speculated that he was born on 22 April on the grounds that his granddaughter, Elizabeth Bernard, chose that date in 1626 for her marriage; the date would, he supposed, 'be celebrated as a festival in the family for generations.'

IS IT TRUE?

No one knows for certain, but it is perfectly possible

You can visit Shakespeare's Birthplace without leaving Japan

The Shakespeare Village at Maruyama-machi, some 75 miles distant from Tokyo, includes reconstructions of Shakespeare's Birthplace, Palmer's Farm (formerly known as Mary Arden's House), and New Place (not available in England), along with a village green, a windmill and a formal garden.

VERDICT

True (if you don't mind a reconstruction)

His father was a Roman Catholic

What is the evidence?

This is a tricky one. John Shakespeare was born probably before 1530, before the English Reformation, and so would have received a Roman Catholic upbringing. The question is whether he retained, or reverted to, his Roman Catholic faith at a time when it would have been both illegal and highly inconvenient to do so, and thus that William may have been brought up in a covertly Roman Catholic household.

There is nothing inherently implausible about this. Throughout the sixteenth century and beyond, Roman Catholics practised their faith in Warwickshire and in many other parts of the country, sometimes secretly, sometimes openly, risking prosecution and persecution. Many recusants, as they were called, paid a monthly fine rather than attend Protestant services. So if John Shakespeare was a crypto-Roman Catholic, he was not alone.

But was he? His children were all baptized, and he was buried in 1601, with Anglican rites. He accepted public office, as, successively, burgess, alderman, and bailiff – mayor – of Stratford-upon-Avon which would have made it impossible for him to avoid attending church services at that time. Under his auspices as Acting Chamberlain in 1564, the painted images in the Guild Chapel were ordered to be defaced as part of the process of change from Roman Catholicism to Protestantism, and in 1571, as chief alderman, he attended the council meeting at which it was ordered that Romish vestments and copes remaining in the Guild Chapel should be sold off. In 1592, however, after he had fallen on relatively hard times, he was in trouble for not attending church services. It was reported that this was because he feared that if he showed himself in public he would have been in danger of being prosecuted for debt. The alternative theory is that he was a recusant. But two certificates issued by the Commissioners for recusancy in Warwickshire in 1592 distinguish clearly between those suspected of absence from church services for religious reasons and those suspected because there they might easily be served with warrants for their arrest, and in both lists John is among those of whom 'It is said that [they] come not to church for fear of process for debt.'

The principal support for the belief that John was a recusant is a document of uncertain provenance known as the Borromeo testament. The first evidence of its existence dates from 1789 when the vicar of Stratford, James Davenport, told the scholar Edmond Malone of a six-leaf manuscript lacking its opening which is now referred to as the Spiritual Last Will and Testament of John Shakespeare. We now know that it derives from the 'Last Will of the Soul, made in health for the Christian to secure himself from the temptations of the devil at the hour of death' composed, probably in the 1570s, by Cardinal Carlo Borromeo at a time of terrible plague. It is assumed that John Shakespeare acquired a copy of this formulaic document, filled his name in the blanks (or, since he appears not to have been able to write, got someone else to do it for him), and hid it (though the final paragraph asserts the writer's intention to carry it continually about him and to have it buried with him.) Malone, assured by Davenport of the authenticity of the Stratford version of this document, decided to print it. In 1790 the Stratford poet and wheelwright John Jordan, who also acted as a self-appointed purveyor of Shakespearian anecdote and legend, sent Malone a collection of papers concerned with Shakespeare which included a manuscript copy of the will. This had now acquired a manuscript opening clearly invented by Jordan, who claimed that in 1757 a master-bricklayer, Joseph Mosely, had found the will in the rafters of John Shakespeare's house. However, suspicion about its authenticity is cast by the fact that Jordan invented its opening.

IS IT TRUE?

Doubts about the reliability of John Jordan inevitably cloud the issue.

VERDICT

I am highly sceptical

HIS FATHER COULDN'T WRITE

WHAT'S THE EVIDENCE?

John Shakespeare was a prominent townsman, a member of the Town Council, an alderman, and bailiff – mayor – in 1568. He was also for many years a successful business man. Yet no scrap of handwriting by him survives. Instead of signing a document he made his mark – a cross or a pair of glover's compasses. Especially since we have much handwriting of Stratford men who held similar positions in the town, it seems clear that Shakespeare's father could not write. But since he kept the borough accounts for over three years he must have been able to read sums, at least. It was not uncommon for people to be able to read but not to write.

VERDICT

True

HIS MOTHER DID NOT LIVE IN THE HOUSE NOW KNOWN AS MARY ARDEN'S HOUSE

WHAT IS THE EVIDENCE?

A tradition going back to the late eighteenth century identified a timber-framed farmhouse in Wilmcote, a small village a few miles north of Stratford, as the one-time property of Robert Arden, Shakespeare's mother's father, and therefore her likely home before her marriage. The Shakespeare Birthplace Trust bought it in 1930 and exhibited it as Mary Arden's House until 2000. In that year, however, by a remarkable piece of research, it was discovered that Robert Arden actually owned a neighbouring house, known as Glebe Farm, and that the so-called Mary Arden's house had belonged to a farmer named Adam Palmer. Happily Glebe Farm already belonged to the Birthplace Trust, and it is now exhibited as the true Mary Arden's House.

VERDICT

Not true, since 2000

His mother couldn't write

What is the evidence?

There was little if any provision for the education of country-born females of the working classes in Shakespeare's time. Mary Arden seems to have been an exceptionally capable woman, since her father chose her as executor of his will in preference to her seven elder sisters, her two stepbrothers, and her two stepsisters when she was still in her teens, and left her a substantial property. She would have had less need to write than her husband, though even women were often required to witness legal documents. On a deed conveying interest in an estate to her nephew Robert Webbe of 1579, she made her mark; it looks like her initials – M S – reversed. The fact that it is not just a scrawl or a pictogram may indicate that she was not unaccustomed to forming letters with a pen.

Verdict

Unproven

HIS DAUGHTERS COULDN'T WRITE

WHAT IS THE EVIDENCE?

His elder daughter, Susanna, signed her name on two legal documents now in the collections of the Shakespeare Birthplace Trust, but her sister Judith made only her mark when she witnessed a deed in 1611, so presumably she could not write.

VERDICT

Not true of Susanna; probably true of Judith

He couldn't spell his own name

What is the evidence?

His surviving signatures vary in spelling.

Is it true?

In an amusing episode in the film *Shakespeare in Love*, he is shown practising various ways of spelling his name. Spelling was very fluid in this period, and the forms of names were not standardized, even on legal documents. At least eighty-three spellings of the name Shakespeare are recorded in documents relating to John Shakespeare. Some of the weirder ones are Shakisspere, Shax'spere, Sakesper, Shasper, and Chacsper. Six surviving signatures of William are generally thought to be authentic: three on his will, one on a document referring to a law case, and two on the documents about his purchase in 1613 of a gatehouse in the Blackfriars area of London. Some are abbreviated, but it looks as if when he wrote his name in full he was most likely to spell it Shakspeare.

Verdict

Not true by the standards of the time

HE GREW UP AT POLESWORTH, NEAR COVENTRY

WHO SAYS SO?

In *A Chapter in the Early Life of Shakespeare* (1926), Arthur Gray, Master of Jesus College, Cambridge, and author of a collection of ghost stories, claimed that at the age of 8 Shakespeare's father sent him to serve as a page to Sir Henry Goodere at Polesworth Hall, in Warwickshire. Here Shakespeare is supposed to have learnt Latin, perhaps to have taught for a while, and then to have been introduced by Goodere to the Earl of Southampton. Gray seems to have been inspired by the fact that the poet and playwright Michael Drayton did actually serve happily as a page at Polesworth.

VERDICT

'It is astonishing that Gray managed to spin a whole book out of his crack-brained thesis; more astonishing still that a distinguished university press (Cambridge) should have published it.' (Schoenbaum)

As a young man, he poached deer at Charlecote

There are several fairly early versions of this popular legend. A Gloucestershire clergyman, Richard Davies, vicar of Sapperton, which is not all that far from Stratford, who died in 1708, wrote in rough manuscript notes that Shakespeare was 'much given to all unluckiness in stealing venison and rabbits, particularly from Sir — Lucy, who had him oft whipped and sometimes imprisoned, and at last made him fly his native country to his great advancement; but his revenge was so great that he is his Justice Clodpate and calls him a great man and that in allusion to his name bore three louses rampant for his arms.' Sir Thomas Lucy was the owner of Charlecote House, close to Stratford. 'Justice Clodpate' clearly refers to Justice Shallow in the opening scene of *The Merry Wives of Windsor*, which contains multiple puns on the word louse, or luce – a kind of fish – which figures in the coat of arms of the Lucy family (among others.)

A less sensational, independent account is provided in Nicholas Rowe's account of Shakespeare's life.

> He had, by a misfortune common enough to young fellows, fallen into ill company; and amongst them, some that made a frequent practice of deer-stealing engaged him with them more than once in robbing a park that belonged to Sir Thomas Lucy of Charlecote, near Stratford. For this he was prosecuted by that gentleman, as he thought, somewhat too severely, and in order to

revenge that ill usage he made a ballad upon him, and though this, probably the first essay of his poetry, be lost, yet it is said to have been so very bitter that it redoubled the prosecution against him to that degree that he was obliged to leave his business and family in Warwickshire for some time, and shelter himself in London.

The story has often been elaborated.

Is it true?

There is no contemporary record of it in legal or any other documents, as we might expect if Shakespeare had really been imprisoned. And *The Merry Wives of Windsor* was written a good many years after Shakespeare started living mainly in London. On the other hand the prevalence of the story in several different and independent accounts suggests that there may be fire behind this smoke.

Verdict

Could be true, up to a point

HE LOVED A WOMAN CALLED ANNE WHATELEY

See p. 160

He had a shotgun wedding

What are the facts?

Shakespeare's marriage licence was issued on 27 November 1582; his first child, Susanna, was baptized less than six months later, on 26 May 1583. ('Fie fie', wrote the essayist Thomas de Quincey, 'you came rather before you were wanted.') This means that – unless the baby was dangerously premature – Anne was pregnant at the time of her marriage. The special licence allowed marriage after only one asking of the banns, which were forbidden from 2 December to 13 January. This suggests a degree of urgency, which would be explained by Anne's pregnancy. Sex before marriage was an offence for which the culprits could be required to do penance in church even after they were married. Shakespeare appears to have escaped this humiliation, but for example in January 1625 a Stratford man, John Davis, was accused of fornication with Elizabeth Wheeler, whom he married by the end of the month, but in March he was brought before the ecclesiastical court 'for begetting his wife with child before marriage.' He and his wife were required to acknowledge their sin in church. This is a situation that Shakespeare dramatizes in *Measure for Measure*, though there the punishment imposed on Claudio for pre-nuptial fornication is execution.

Verdict

Probably true

HE WAS MARRIED AT LUDDINGTON

It seems likely that Shakespeare's marriage did not take place in Stratford, as it is not recorded in the town's registers. A writer called S. W. Fullom, in his *History of William Shakespeare*, of 1862, wrote of the vicarage of Luddington, a small village close to Stratford, that

> The house is occupied by a family named Dyke, respected for miles round, and here the report of the marriage can be traced back directly for a hundred and fifty years. Mrs Dyke received it from Martha Casebrooke, who died at the age of ninety, after residing her whole life in the village, and not only declared that she was told in her childhood that the marriage was solemnized at Luddington, but had seen the ancient tome in which it was registered. This, indeed, we found, on visiting the neighbouring cottages, was remembered by persons still living, when it was in the possession of a Mrs Pickering, who had been housekeeper to Mr Coles, the last curate; and one day burnt the register to boil her kettle!

As Schoenbaum writes, 'This account is sufficiently circumstantial to suggest at least the possibility of a true report.'

VERDICT

May be true

HE WAS MARRIED AT TEMPLE GRAFTON

This is one of the 'Shakespeare Villages' *(see p. 72)*, a few miles from Stratford. On her marriage, Anne Hathaway was described as being 'of Temple Grafton', although she is known to have come from Shottery. A possible explanation is that she was married there, though there is no other evidence to that effect. The vicar was an eccentric clergyman named John Frith, who is described in a Puritan survey of 1576 – six years previously – as 'an old priest, and unsound in religion' – which probably implies that he had Roman Catholic sympathies. It was said that he 'can neither preach nor read well', and that his 'chiefest trade is to cure hawks that are hurt or diseased, for which purpose many do usually repair to him.'

VERDICT

Maybe, again

THE LOST YEARS

WHAT ARE THEY?

This name is often given to the period of Shakespeare's early manhood when we don't know how he was earning a living. Except for a passing mention in a court case of 1587, there is no documented reference to him between the baptism of his twins, Hamnet and Judith, in Stratford-upon-Avon on 2 February 1585, when he was 20, and the unfriendly allusion to him in the pamphlet *Greene's Groatsworth of Wit* (*see p. 161*) in 1592, when he was 26. He must have begun his career as both actor and writer during this time, but no one knows when. The question is how he was employed before he got involved with the theatre. There have been many guesses, some more sensible than others.

HE LIVED FOR A TIME IN LANCASHIRE

WHO SAYS SO?

The theory first appeared in 1937. It grew in popularity towards the end of the twentieth century, partly under the influence of a book by E. A. J. Honigmann called *Shakespeare: the Lost Years* (1985). The idea is that soon after leaving school Shakespeare went to Lancashire, possibly under the influence of, or with, John Cottam, who taught at the Stratford grammar school from September 1579 to late in 1581 or early in 1582 and then returned to his family home at Tarnacre, near where Hoghton lived.

WHAT IS THE EVIDENCE?

It comes from the will of a wealthy Roman Catholic landowner, Alexander Hoghton, of 1581. In it he leaves to his half-brother, Thomas Hoghton, 'all my instruments belonging to musics, and all manner of play clothes, if he be minded to keep and do keep players, and if he will not keep and maintain players then it is my mind and will that Sir Thomas Hesketh knight shall have the same instruments and play clothes, and I most heartily require the said Sir Thomas to be friendly unto Foke [i.e. Fulke] Gyllom and William Shakeshafte, now dwelling with me, and either to take them unto his service, or else to help them to some good master.'

IS IT TRUE?

There are various objections to it. Shakeshaft is not the same name as Shakespeare, and although the spelling and forms of names were fluid in the period, it is interesting that Shakeshaft was a very common name in Lancashire but is not found in Warwickshire. Supporters of the theory build on Aubrey's report that Shakespeare was 'a schoolmaster in the country' (p. 42) to suppose that for some reason he preceded Cottam to Lancashire as a tutor in the Hoghton household, though the will does not imply that Shakeshaft was a teacher, or even necessarily a musician or player, or that it was the Lancashire countryside in which he taught.

VERDICT

I am very sceptical

HE WAS A ROMAN CATHOLIC

WHO SAYS SO?

This idea seems to have been first put forward by the Protestant Richard Davies *(see also p. 31)* in the late seventeenth century. Writing of Shakespeare's monument, he adds 'He died a papist.' Over the years the belief has frequently been revived, especially in connection with the theory that Shakespeare is the William Shakeshaft mentioned in Alexander Hoghton's will in 1581 *(see p. 38)*. A recent proponent is Clare Asquith, in her book *Shadowplay: The Hidden Beliefs and Coded Politics of William Shakespeare* (2005). She argues that Shakespeare 'developed a series of code words that remain the same throughout his work and give the reader unerring compass bearings to the hidden dramas. These simple code words, some of them shared by fellow writers, include terms for Protestantism, Catholicism, England, the queen, the Reformation, the Catholic powers abroad, the underground resistance. They provide the basis for a range of more fleeting topical allusions, many of them brilliantly ingenious, some of them intensely poignant.'

IS IT TRUE?

It relates to similar theories about his father *(see p. 22)*, and is open to some of the same objections. All Shakespeare's life records – baptism, marriage, baptisms of his children, burial of his father and mother, purchase of tithes, his own burial, grave and monument in Holy Trinity – suggest that he was a conforming member of the Established Church – a mainstream

Protestant. The problem with Clare Asquith's 'code' is that it is of her own invention – the words in which she finds hidden and arbitrary meanings have surface meanings that require no further elucidation. As she herself says, 'The essence of this coded method of writing, of course, was that it be "deniable" – in other words, incapable of proof' (p. xiv). It remains as incapable of proof today as it was in Shakespeare's time.

It is incidentally worth remembering that some of Shakespeare's contemporaries, such as Ben Jonson, converted from Protestantism to Catholicism and back again.

VERDICT

Unlikely

HE WAS A SCHOOLMASTER
IN THE COUNTRY

This legend goes back to John Aubrey, who in his *Brief Lives*, after remarking that Ben Jonson says 'he had but little Latin and less Greek', nevertheless adds 'he understood Latin pretty well, for he had been in his younger years a schoolmaster in the country.' A marginal note indicates that he had this information 'from Mr Beeston' (William Beeston, son of Christopher, an actor in Shakespeare's company.) This appears to be good, if indirect, authority, but Aubrey is notoriously unreliable. Lacking a university degree Shakespeare could not have had charge of a school, but it is not impossible that he worked for a while as an assistant teacher — an 'usher' — in a school.

Is it true?

Not impossible

He worked in a lawyer's office

Who says so?

The great scholar and editor Edmond Malone (1741-1812), who had trained as a barrister, suggested that during the 'lost years' Shakespeare may have worked in a lawyer's office. The idea has been taken up by a number of later writers.

What is the evidence?

It is a deduction from the knowledge of the law displayed in the vocabulary of Shakespeare's works and in his recorded dealings with the law.

Is it true?

It is subject to the same criticism as the other theories based purely, or largely, on evidence extrapolated from the plays. Shakespeare was widely read and no doubt had many experiences that found their way into the language of his plays, but that does not necessarily mean that he was a member of the professions on whose terminology he drew.

Verdict

Not proven

HE WAS A SEAMAN

WHO SAYS SO?

In *The Real Shakespeare, A Counterblast to Commentators* (1947), the 82-year-old William Bliss, known as 'the father of English canoeing', proposed that when Shakespeare was 13 he left home to join Sir Francis Drake on his voyage round the world on the *Golden Hind*, as demonstrated by the reference to 'remainder biscuit' in *As You Like It*. Ships' biscuits were apparently carried only on very long voyages. In 1585, Bliss claimed, Shakespeare went to sea again, was shipwrecked on the coast of Illyria (the setting for *Twelfth Night*), and found his way from there to Venice where he met and fell in love with the Earl of Southampton.

The principal later statement of the theory is in a book called *Shakespeare and the Sea*, by A. F. Falconer, published in 1964. Falconer was a Professor of English at St Andrew's University who had also served in the navy. He argues that Shakespeare's knowledge of the sea as displayed in, for example, the opening scene of *The Tempest* was so extensive and precise that it could have been gained only from direct personal experience.

IS IT TRUE?

Again, the plays are full of information and terminology that Shakespeare could have acquired without personal experience of the professions and trades with which they are associated.

VERDICT

Not true

HE WAS A SOLDIER

WHO SAYS SO?

The principal exponent of this idea was Duff Cooper (1890-1954), first Viscount Norwich, who joined the Foreign Office and served briefly but with distinction in the army during the First World War. He later had a successful career in politics. In 1949 he published *Sergeant Shakespeare*, a short, gracefully written book in the form of a letter addressed to his wife, Lady Diana Cooper. In it he speculates that Shakespeare, after the birth of his twins in 1585, followed the Earl of Leicester on his campaign to the Netherlands. He quotes a letter from Sir Philip Sidney – who died on the campaign – saying 'I wrote you a letter by [i. e. carried by] Will, my Lord of Leicester's jesting player ....', and suggests that Will is Shakespeare. Cooper surveys the roles of soldiers in the plays, noting the 'sympathy and understanding with which they are presented.' At the end he writes 'Have I convinced you? I have almost convinced myself.'

VERDICT

He hasn't convinced me, either

His first job in the theatre was holding the heads of horses for patrons

Who says so?

This is a late anecdote, told by Dr Samuel Johnson in 1765. He says that

> Many came on horseback to the play, and when Shakespeare fled to London from the terror of a criminal prosecution, his first expedient was to wait at the door of the playhouse and hold the horses of those that had no servants, that they might be ready again after the performance.

According to Johnson he carried out his duties with exemplary zeal, became very popular in this role, and went into business, hiring boys to work under his direction.

Johnson seems unlikely to have made the story up himself, but there is no clue as to where he got it from. He said it had been told by Nicholas Rowe to Alexander Pope, but it is suspicious that neither made use of it.

Verdict

Probably not true

HE WAS AN ACTOR

WHAT IS THE EVIDENCE?

The clearest objective evidence is the presence of his name in printed character lists for Ben Jonson's *Every Man in his Humour* (acted in 1598) and *Sejanus* (printed in 1603), and in the list in his own First Folio (1623) headed 'The Names of the Principal Actors in All these Plays.' His name comes first in this list, presumably simply because he is the author.

VERDICT

True

HE ACTED THE GHOST IN *Hamlet* AND ADAM IN *As You Like It*

Nicholas Rowe, in his account of Shakespeare's life published in his 1709 edition of the Complete Plays, said that 'the top of his performance was the Ghost in his own *Hamlet*.' Rowe made genuine efforts to learn about Shakespeare's life, so this could be true. It's not a star role (though Bernard Shaw, writing that 'the Ghost's part is one of the wonders of the play', declared this to be 'the reason why Shakespear [sic] would not trust anyone else with it.')

The story about Adam is even less well authenticated. The herald and antiquarian William Oldys (1696-1761) wrote that one of Shakespeare's younger brothers, having lived into the Restoration, told actors of the time in his very old age that he remembered 'having once seen [his brother] act a part in one of his own comedies, wherein being to personate a decrepit old man, he wore a long beard, and appeared so weak and drooping and unable to walk, that he was forced to be supported and carried by another person to a table, at which he was seated among some company, who were eating, and one of them sung a song.' This obviously refers to Adam in *As You Like It*, but the validity of the story is negated by the fact that none of Shakespeare's brothers lived into the Restoration.

VERDICT

The Ghost, possible; Adam, no worthwhile evidence

HE NEGLECTED HIS WIFE AND CHILDREN

WHAT IS THE EVIDENCE?

This judgement reflects the sketchiness of our knowledge about Shakespeare's adult life. As a member of the theatrical profession he had to base himself in London. We know that he lived in several different lodgings there in the 1590s and later. There is no evidence that he took his wife and children with him, or even that they ever visited him there (though they may have done.) On the other hand there is much to show that he provided amply for them in Stratford, where he bought a grand house and garden in 1597, when he was only thirty-three years old. At various points in his lifetime he bought more property and land in and near his home town. How often he returned home it is impossible to say. The family stuck together, and his will shows that he was anxious to make provision for his widow, his two daughters, and for other members of his family.

COMMENT

Certainly he often lived away from home for long periods. Whether this counts as enforced separation, as a decision which may have been carefully considered and more or less cheerfully accepted on both sides, or as neglect is impossible to say.

VERDICT

We don't know

He was a womanizer

There is an anecdote that has come down in two closely related versions. One is from the eighteenth century, in a book called *A General View of the English Stage* (1759), by Thomas Wilkes. He writes:

> One evening when *Richard III* was to be performed, Shakespeare observed a young woman delivering a message to Burbage in so cautious a manner as excited his curiosity to listen to. It imported that her master was gone out of town that morning, and her mistress would be glad of his company after play, and to know what signal he would appoint for admittance. Burbage replied 'Three taps at the door, and "It is I, Richard the Third."' She immediately withdrew, and Shakespeare followed till he observed her to go into a house in the city; and enquiring in the neighbourhood, he was informed that a young lady lived there, the favourite of an old rich merchant. Near the appointed time of meeting, Shakespeare thought proper to anticipate Mr Burbage, and was introduced by the concerted signal. The lady was very much surprised at Shakespeare's presuming to act Mr Burbage's part, but as he – who had wrote *Romeo and Juliet* –, we may be certain, did not want wit or eloquence to apologize for the intrusion, she was soon pacified, and they were mutually happy till Burbage came to the door and repeated the same signal; but Shakespeare popping his head out of the window, bid him be gone, for that William the Conqueror had reigned before Richard III.

This is an elaborated version of a joke which clearly circulated in Shakespeare's time. The copious diaries and notebooks of

John Manningham (c. 1575-1622), a Cambridge graduate who studied law at the Middle Temple, include the following entry for 13 March 1602:

> Upon a time when Burbage played Richard the Third there was a citizen grew so far in liking with him, that before she went from the play she appointed him to come that night unto her by the name of Richard the Third. Shakespeare, overhearing their conclusion, went before, was entertained and at his game ere Burbage came. Then, message being brought that Richard the Third was at the door, Shakespeare caused return to be made that William the Conqueror was before Richard the Third.

Manningham claims to have had this story from a colleague, William Touse. Manningham had seen a performance of Shakespeare's play *Twelfth Night* in the hall of the Middle Temple a few weeks earlier, on 2 February 1602.

Wilkes cannot have got the anecdote from Manningham's diaries as they remained unpublished until the nineteenth century. The existence of two independent witnesses does not prove that it is true, only that it seemed a good enough joke to be worth circulating.

IS THERE ANYTHING TO BACK UP THE IDEA?

Shakespeare's Sonnets (some of which may or may not be autobiographical) include a number of poems addressed to or concerning a woman (or possibly more than one woman) whom the poet writes of as black and whom later ages have referred to as 'the dark lady' with whom he had what was clearly an adulterous affair. Furthermore, in Sonnet 31 the poet writes of 'trophies of my lovers gone' (which could refer to either male or female lovers.) Shakespeare must often have been apart from his wife for months on end when he was on tour and working in London, and there are lots of stories about women theatre-goers of the period (as of every other period) having assignations with actors, so maybe it wouldn't be surprising if he had girl friends.

VERDICT

Probably true, up to a point

HE WAS GAY

WHO SAID IT FIRST?

We can't say exactly, but it goes back a long way, mainly because some of his sonnets are addressed to a young male, whom he refers to as, for instance, 'my lovely boy' (Sonnet 126). This seems to have embarrassed the publisher John Benson, because when he first reprinted the sonnets, in 1640, he unsystematically changed a few of the pronouns and added titles to some of the poems making them look as if they referred to a woman rather than a man. Since then many writers have supposed that Shakespeare must have been in love with the young man, or young men, of the Sonnets.

IS IT TRUE?

He married and had children. Some of the sonnets – which are his most personal writings – express deep love and yearning for a man. There is no clear evidence that he had sexual relations with a male. But it looks as if he felt deep love for one or more young men, and this could have found physical expression.

VERDICT

Not proven

HE HAD AN AFFAIR WITH THE EARL OF SOUTHAMPTON

WHO SAYS SO?

The idea that Southampton was Shakespeare's 'bosom-friend' was first mooted by Nathan Drake in his vast, two-volume work *Shakespeare and his Times* (1817). It finds exuberant modern expression in Erica Jong's novel *Serenissima* (1987)

IS IT TRUE?

Henry Wriothesley, third Earl of Southampton, was born in 1573, making him about eleven years younger than Shakespeare. He was a brilliant and beautiful young man of many talents and interests. In 1593, Shakespeare dedicated to him his narrative poem *Venus and Adonis*. It was customary at this period for poets to write dedications to noble patrons. In return they usually received a gift of money — two guineas (£2.2.0) was a common sum — and may also have received other favours, such as the use of a library or hospitality. The dedication to *Venus and Adonis* is relatively formal. In the following year, however, Shakespeare dedicated his second narrative poem, *The Rape of Lucrece*, also to Southampton. These two long poems are the only works by Shakespeare that he seems himself to have been responsible for publishing. This time the dedication is couched in much warmer terms, suggesting that an unusually affectionate relationship had grown up between the poet and his patron. 'The love I dedicate to your lordship is without end. … What I have done is yours, what I have to do is yours, being part in all I have, devoted yours.' Shakespeare dedicated no other of his works to a patron.

There are other links. Also in 1594, Shakespeare's play *The Comedy of Errors* was performed in, and possibly written for, Gray's Inn, an inn of court (law school) of which Southampton was a member. Conceivably he commissioned it. In 1709 Nicholas Rowe wrote that the Earl of Southampton gave Shakespeare £1000. The Earl was extravagant, but this is so large a sum that it is difficult to believe. Still, there is contemporary evidence that Southampton was sexually attracted to males, most blatantly in a letter written in 1599 – by which time he was married to Elizabeth Vernon – which reports that when the Earl was on military service in Ireland with the Earl of Essex, he had what was regarded as an unseemly relationship with one Captain Piers Edmonds. The letter writer says that Edmonds 'ate and drank at his table, and lay in his tent, the Earl of Southampton gave him a horse, which Edmunds refused a hundred marks for him [i.e. it was very valuable]. The Earl Southampton would clip and hug him in his arms and play wantonly with him.' It is reasonable to suppose that Shakespeare had a genuine friendship with Southampton, in spite of the differences in their age and social status; but of course the word 'love' in the dedication to *Lucrece* does not necessarily imply a physical relationship.

The other, much more tenuous but also more suggestive link is with the Sonnets. In some of these a young man is described in terms which might be used of Southampton's appearance in his portraits. In view of the known links between the two men, it is at least conceivable that Shakespeare is writing of, and to, Southampton.

A further complication is the dedication to the 1609 publication of the Sonnets to 'Mr W. H.', who is said to be the poems' 'only begetter.' This time the dedication is written not by Shakespeare but by the publisher, Thomas Thorpe, whose initials stand at the end of it. 'W. H.' are Southampton's initials reversed; he was not properly addressed as 'Mr.' If it is a reference to him, it is a cryptic one, but then the very use of initials here is itself cryptic – a way, it would seem, of hinting identity to those in the know while concealing it from the rest of the world.

Overall it is fair to say that a) when Shakespeare was in his early thirties he had a warm friendship with the young Earl; b) the Earl must have reciprocated this to have permitted the second dedication; c) there are possible links between the Earl and the young man of the sonnets.

VERDICT

Friendship: yes. Anything more: not proven

*This androgynous-looking portrait of the Earl of Southampton,
identified only in 2000, was previously believed to represent a woman,
Lady Norton.*

He had an affair with the Countess of Southampton

Who says so?

This theory originated with Professor Hildegard Hammer-schmidt-Hummel, a prolific creator of Shakespearian myths.

What is the argument?

In Hampton Court Palace there is a fine painting by Marcus Gheeraerts the Younger (1562-1636) known as 'The Persian Lady' which has attracted much attention from art historians and others. It shows a pregnant lady richly dressed in Persian costume comforting a wounded stag. It also features a tree, a motto, and a sonnet which relates to the subject matter of the painting. Over the years there has been much speculation about the identity of the sitter and the purpose of the painting, which is clearly emblematic. Among the more bizarre theories has been the idea that it shows Queen Elizabeth illegitimately pregnant with either Francis Bacon or Henry Wriothesley, Earl of Southampton. More convincingly, Sir Roy Strong has argued that it shows Frances Walsingham, Countess of Essex, that it was painted in 1600 as an appeal to the Queen on behalf of Essex and his wife, who gave birth to a daughter in December 1600, and that the stag represents Essex after his defeat in Ireland (he was to be executed in the following year). The wounded stag motif relates to a speech by Jaques in *As You Like*, written around this time; but it was a commonplace, derived from Ovid.

The sonnet – not a bad poem – refers to both a tree and a stag. In 1999 Hammerschmidt-Hummel argued that the sonnet is by Shakespeare, that the woman is therefore the 'dark lady', and that Shakespeare is therefore the father of the unborn child. She further claimed, on the basis of alleged resemblances among other paintings backed up by the testimony of 'forensic scientists', that the woman is Elizabeth Vernon, who became the wife of Henry Wriothesley, third Earl of Southampton (*see p. 54*). She had been pregnant before her marriage, and her husband is said to have behaved coldly towards their daughter, Penelope. From this Hammerschmidt-Hummel deduces that the father of the child was not actually the Earl but her supposed lover, William Shakespeare, claiming that a portrait of Penelope resembles Shakespeare rather the Southampton.

IS IT TRUE?

Need you ask?

HE HAD AN AFFAIR WITH WILLIAM HERBERT, THIRD EARL OF PEMBROKE

WHO SAYS SO?

The idea that Herbert is the 'lovely boy' of the Sonnets was first mooted by the biographer James Boaden in his book *On the Sonnets of Shakespeare: Identifying the Person to Whom They Are Addressed, and Elucidating several Points in the Poet's History* (1837), expanded from an article of 1832. The theory is still often espoused, for example by Katherine Duncan-Jones in her Arden edition of the sonnets and in the BBC television film *A Waste of Shame* (2005), scripted by William Boyd, on which she advised.

WHAT IS THE EVIDENCE?

William Herbert was born in 1580, making him 16 years younger than Shakespeare. He was a keen and generous patron of the arts, including the drama. This is reflected in the dedication by Shakespeare's fellow actors John Heminges and Henry Condell jointly to him and to his brother, Philip, of the Shakespeare First Folio, in 1623, seven years after Shakespeare died. There are no indisputable biographical links between him and Shakespeare. The theory that they had a close relationship rests mainly on Thomas Thorpe's dedication of the Sonnets in 1609 to 'Mr W. H' *(see pp. 56 and 163)*. Like Southampton, Herbert would not properly have been addressed as Mr; on the other hand these are his initials, and in the right order. The idea that he is the young man addressed in some of the sonnets has been fostered by the fact that the first seventeen of those poems urge the person addressed to marry and to have a child, and that in his young manhood Herbert refused several proffered brides.

Is it true?

Herbert attended plays at court, and was deeply distressed by the death in 1619 of Richard Burbage, the leading actor of Shakespeare's company. Heminges and Condell dedicated the First Folio jointly to Herbert and to his brother, the Earl of Montgomery; Shakespeare must have known him as an enthusiastic theatregoer. But there is no clear evidence of a close personal relationship between the two men.

Verdict

Unlikely

William Davenant was Shakespeare's illegitimate son / godson

Who was he?

Sir William Davenant (1606-68) was a poet, playwright, and theatre manager who played a major role in the transition from the closing of London's theatres during the period when they were closed by the Puritans, in 1640, to their re-opening when King Charles II came to the throne, in 1660. He adapted several of Shakespeare's plays to make them suitable for the much-changed conditions of the Restoration playhouses, with women actors, representational scenery, and so on. He was brought up in Oxford, where his father, a keen theatre-goer, kept a successful tavern, The Golden Cross (now in part a Pizza Express restaurant.) John Aubrey, who was a friend of Davenant, says in his *Brief Lives* that Davenant thought he wrote with Shakespeare's spirit, and was happy to call himself his son. This has led to the supposition that Shakespeare had an affair with Davenant's mother on his journeys between Stratford and London, but there is no real evidence for this, and 'son' could mean simply a follower or disciple: disciples of Ben Jonson were known as the 'sons of Ben.' There are also reports that Shakespeare was Davenant's godfather; this is possible – they share the same, admittedly very common, forename – but seems unlikely as Shakespeare leaves a bequest in his will to his god-son William Walker, but not to Davenant.

Verdict

Unlikely

He smoked cannabis

Who says so?

In 1999 Professor Francis Thackeray, of the University of the Transvaal, was reported to have come to the conclusion that Shakespeare smoked cannabis. He was said to have analysed remains of clay pipes found in Stratford, some of which showed traces of the drug. He bolstered his claim by quoting the phrase 'invention in a noted weed' (Sonnet 76).

What are the arguments against it?

There is no proof that the pipes belonged to Shakespeare. And the word 'weed' in Sonnet 76 clearly refers to costume, as in 'These your unusual weeds.' (*The Winter's Tale*, 4.4.1)

Verdict

Pure fiction

HE NEVER TRAVELLED OVERSEAS

The majority of Shakespeare's plays have overseas settings – Italy, France, Cyprus, Denmark, Bohemia, Sicily, and so on – but for him (as for Queen Elizabeth I), there is no clear evidence that he ever travelled outside the British Isles. It is often conjectured that he must at least have travelled to Italy, where many plays are set, but no one has ever succeeded in showing that they contain information that he could not have acquired either from books or from conversation with travellers. Some English actors travelled in Europe, but there is no evidence that Shakespeare was among them.

VERDICT

Probably true

HE COULD READ/SPEAK ITALIAN

Many of his plays are set, either in whole or in part, in Italy. Around six of them incorporate occasional words or phrases in Italian. In itself this is not enough to show that Shakespeare could read or speak the language – he might have picked them up from other reading, or in conversation. There are however two reasons to suppose that he could read Italian. One is that at a few points in his plays he writes dialogue that appears to be influenced by passages that were available to him only in that language. An example is in *Othello*, where Iago says:

> You are pictures out of door,
> Bells in your parlours; wildcats in your kitchens,
> Saints in your injuries; devils being offended,
> Players in your housewifery, and hussies in your beds.

> (2.1.112–115)

This seems to derive from a passage printed admittedly in both English and Italian in an Italian-English instruction book published in 1591 and called *Second Fruits* by John Florio, whom Shakespeare may well have known (*see p. 137*).

More importantly, some of Shakespeare's plays depend for their plots on Italian writings that had not been translated into English. *The Merchant of Venice* draws on *Il Pecorone* (1558), by Ser Giovanni Fiorentino, which had not been translated into any other language by the time Shakespeare wrote his play. *Measure for Measure* depends in part on *Hecatommithi*, by Giraldi Cinthio, first published in 1558, and on Cinthio's play based on it, *Epitia*, published in 1583, not available in any other language.

Perhaps most significantly, *Othello* is based on another story from Cinthio, which had been translated into French but not into English, and which seems to echo the Italian closely at several points.

VERDICT

'It seems clear, therefore, from plays which have an Italian source that Shakespeare could read Italian, and that for a surprising number of plays he read those sources in Italian.' (Naseeb Shaheen)

HE COULD READ/SPEAK FRENCH

The two foreign languages that Shakespeare draws on most freely are Latin and French. He would have learned Latin at school. Some of the French words and expressions that he uses, such as *monsieur*, *oui*, and *roi*, are commonplace. The clearest evidence that he could read and write in French is the presence in *Henry V* of an entire scene – 3.4 – written in that language.

VERDICT

True

His signet ring survives

Who says so?

In March 1818 the painter Benjamin Robert Haydon wrote breathlessly to his friend John Keats 'I shall certainly go mad! In a field at Stratford upon Avon, in a field that belonged to Shakespeare; they have found a gold ring and seal, with the initial thus — *W. S. and a true lover's knot between*. If *this* is not Shakespeare who is it? — a true lover's knot!! — ... As sure as you breathe, & that he was the first of beings the Seal belonged to him — O Lord! —'. Keats replied with understandable though kindly scepticism.

The ring, now in the possession of The Shakespeare Birthplace Trust, is on exhibition with a cautious caption. The story of its discovery in 1810, eight years before Haydon wrote, is recounted by the Stratford solicitor Robert Bell Wheler in his *Guide to Stratford-upon-Avon* of 1814. The find was made by a labourer's wife named Martin in a field next to the churchyard; oddly — perhaps auspiciously — a man named William Shakespeare was working in the field at the time. The ring was nearly black with rust and although Wheler bought it (for the value of its weight in gold) on the day it was found Mrs Martin had already had time to have it 'unnecessarily immersed in aquafortis to ascertain and prove the metal at a silver-smith's shop, which consequently restored its original colour' but regrettably destroyed what might have been useful evidence in the ring's encrustation. Wheler — a reputable local historian — tells that in spite of 'numerous researches into public and private documents' he found 'no Stratfordian of that period so likely to own such a ring as Shakespeare.' He also intriguingly noted that no seal is affixed to Shakespeare's will but that 'where the Scrivener had written "In witness whereof I have hereunto set my hand and Seal" these words "and seal" were struck out,' as if Shakespeare had recently lost his seal ring. (In fact 'hand' is substituted for 'seal' in the will.) Early in the twentieth century the scholar E. K. Chambers, ever cautious, proposed that the separation of the initials on the ring by a lovers' knot 'may indicate two persons rather than one.' But this ignores the entire function of a seal ring, which is to emboss the initials of an individual on the wax with which a legal or other official document is sealed. The possibility that this ring is the only surviving personal relic of Shakespeare is stronger than has usually been supposed. Michael Wood, in *In Search of Shakespeare* (2003), evolves a picturesquely detailed scenario for what might have happened, conjecturing that Shakespeare 'dropped his signet ring after Judith's wedding ... The ceremony had taken place in February, the coldest month of another very cold winter. He might well have been wearing gloves. He was perhaps already ill, and might have lost weight; the ring could have been loose. Outside the church, after the service, perhaps he took his gloves off to shake hands with an old acquaintance. The ring would easily have fallen off, unnoticed, and been lost.'

VERDICT

Quite possibly true

THERE ARE NO SURVIVING LETTERS EITHER TO OR FROM HIM

It is true that no letters written by Shakespeare survive. There is however one letter addressed to him, now in the collections of The Shakespeare Birthplace Trust. It was written by his fellow-townsman Richard Quiney, whose son was to marry Shakespeare's daughter Judith, and reads:

> Loving countryman, I am bold of you as a friend, craving your help with £30 upon Mr Bushell's and my security or Mr Mytton's with me. Mr Roswell [probably Thomas Russell, a wealthy Warwickshire gentlemen whom Shakespeare was to appoint overseer of his will] is not come to London as yet and I have especial cause. You shall friend me much in helping me out of all the debts I owe in London, I thank God, and much quiet my mind which would not be indebted. I am now towards the court in hope of answer for the dispatch of my business. You shall neither lose credit nor money by me, the Lord willing, and now but persuade yourself so as I hope and you shall not need to fear but with all hearty thankfulness I will hold my time and content your friend and if we bargain further you shall be the paymaster yourself. My time bids me hasten to an end and so I commit this to your care and hope of your help. I fear I shall not be back this night from the court. Haste. The Lord be with you and with us all, Amen.

> From the Bell in Carter Lane, the 25 October [St Crispin's Day, as it happens] 1598.

> Yours in all kindness,

> Ric[hard] Quiney

The Bell was an inn near St Paul's Cathedral, and seems to have been a regular stopping haunt of visitors from Stratford. Its site bears a plaque commemorating the fact that the letter was written there. The letter was found among Quiney's papers, so it appears never to have been sent. Maybe he ran into Shakespeare in person. £30 was a very large sum, and the request indicates that Quiney was confident that Shakespeare had the funds to oblige him. It is possible that Quiney was requesting the cash as a business transaction, perhaps on behalf of the town, on which Shakespeare (who had recently written *The Merchant of Venice*) would receive interest. Quiney was optimistic that Shakespeare would respond favourably, writing to a friend Abraham Sturley in Stratford a few days later of his confidence 'that our countryman Master William Shakespeare would procure us money', but Sturley was sceptical: 'Which I will like of as I shall hear and when, and where, and how.'

IS IT TRUE?

No letters from him; one to him

HE WAS A HEAVY DRINKER

WHO SAYS SO?

There is an eighteenth-century legend, which appeared in *The British Magazine* in 1762, that a crab-apple tree near the village of Bidford, a few miles from Stratford, was known as Shakespeare's Canopy because he had slept under it one night after a bout of heavy drinking. The informant claimed to have the tale from 'two young women, lineal descendants of our great dramatic poet' who kept 'a little ale-house, some small distance from Stratford.' This is clearly untrue, at least in part, since no lineal descendants of Shakespeare were alive after 1670. The story was that having heard that the men of Bidford were famous for the amount they could drink, he decided to compete with them. In a later version, the eighteenth-century Stratford poet John Jordan — a prolific and highly unreliable source of anecdote — claims that on being woken Shakespeare refused to continue the contest, saying that he had drunk with

> Piping Pebworth, Dancing Marston,
> Haunted Hillborough, Hungry Grafton,
> Dadgeing Exhall, Papist Wixford,
> Beggarly Broom, and Drunken Bidford.

These are all villages in the vicinity of Stratford.

A tree was later identified as the one under which Shakespeare had fallen asleep, and was torn to pieces by souvenir hunters.

IS THERE EVIDENCE TO THE CONTRARY?

In the later part of the seventeenth century, John Aubrey wrote that Shakespeare was 'the more to be admired [because] he was not a company keeper lived in Shoreditch, wouldn't be debauched, and if invited to, writ he was in pain.'

IS IT TRUE?

Well, he may have been – though if so he managed to cram in an awful lot of work too; and the eighteenth-century bit of evidence is very dicey.

See also p. 83

VERDICT

Probably not true

HE WAS LAME

WHO SAYS SO?

Edward Capell (1713-81), the great editor, made this deduction on the basis of Sonnet 37, where the poet writes that he has been 'made lame by fortune's spite', and Sonnet 89, 'Speak of my lameness and I straight will halt.' It is subject to two principal objections: it takes what may well be metaphorical language as literal truth; and anyway the Sonnets are not necessarily autobiographical.

VERDICT

No reliable evidence

He had a breakdown around 1608

Who said so?

Sir E. K. Chambers, author of the monumental *Shakespeare: A Study of Facts and Problems* (2 vols., 1930), speculated that

> Shakespeare's spirit had been nearly submerged in *Lear*, and although the wave passed, and he rose to the height of poetic expression in *Antony and Cleopatra*, I think that he went under in the unfinished *Timon of Athens*. The chronology of the plays becomes difficult at this point, and it is therefore frankly a conjecture that an attempt at *Timon of Athens* early in 1608 was followed by a serious illness, which may have been a nervous breakdown, and on the other hand may have been merely [sic] the plague. Later in the year Shakespeare came to his part of *Pericles* with a new outlook. In any case the transition from the tragedies to the romances is not an evolution but a revolution. There has been some mental process such as the psychology of religion would call a conversion.

Is it true?

This is a surprisingly subjective statement to have come from so level-headed and generally objective as scholar as Chambers. There is no external evidence for it whatever. It was countered by Professor C. J. Sisson in his British Academy Lecture 'The Mythical Sorrows of Shakespeare' (1934), in which he writes: 'Shakespeare was not stung into tragedy by any Dark Lady. He was not depressed into tragedy by the fall of Essex, who threatened revolution and chaos in England, to Shakespeare's horror and alarm; the cruelty of anarchy was a thought that haunted the poet like a nightmare. He did not degenerate into tragedy in a semi-delirium of cynicism and melancholy, ending in a religious crisis. Shakespeare *rose* to tragedy in the very height and peak of his powers, nowhere else so splendidly displayed, and maintained throughout his robust and transcendent faith in God and his creature Man.' (This counterblast too is subjective.)

VERDICT

Guesswork: unlikely

WE DON'T KNOW WHAT HE LOOKED LIKE

Let's start with the most positive evidence. The First Folio, printed in 1623, has on its titlepage an engraved portrait by Martin Droeshout:

On the opposite page are lines saying

> This figure that thou here seest put,
>> It was for gentle Shakespeare cut;
> Wherein the graver had a strife
>> With Nature to out-do the life:
> O, could he but have drawn his wit
>> As well in brass as he hath hit
> His face, the print would then surpass
>> All that was ever writ in brass.
> But since he cannot, reader, look
>> Not on his picture but his book .

B. I.

'B. I.' pretty certainly stands for Ben Jonson (the letter j was represented by i), whose great poem in praise of Shakespeare is printed among the early leaves of the book. Moreover the volume was apparently seen through the press by Shakespeare's friends and lifelong colleagues, John Heminges and Henry Condell. All of this suggests that the engraving was a good enough likeness of Shakespeare to pass muster with them. It must have been made from a drawing or painting which has not survived.

Secondly, there is the bust which forms part of Shakespeare's monument in Holy Trinity Church, Stratford-upon-Avon.

This was in place by 1623, at which time many people who had known him well, including his two daughters and his son-in-law, and possibly his widow (who died in that year) were still alive. The bust was restored in the eighteenth century, but there is good evidence that its appearance was not substantially altered, so again we may suppose that it is at least an adequate likeness. It has however been opposed that the bust originally represented John Shakespeare *(see p. 80)*.

Apart from this, a number of paintings have been supposed to offer authentic likenesses of Shakespeare; the only one that is now seriously considered as having possibly been painted from life is that known as the Chandos portrait, now in the National Portrait Gallery.

VERDICT

Not true

The monument in Holy Trinity Church originally represented Shakespeare's father, not Shakespeare himself

Who says so?

This idea seems first to have emerged in 2006 on a web-site run by Richard Kennedy, who claims 'The monument as first conceived and erected, featured a man with his hands resting on an emblematic woolpack, a proper tribute to a renown [sic] civic father and newly made gentleman, John Shakspeare, "a considerable dealer in wool."' Its basis is a sketch made in 1634, eighteen years after the poet died, by William Dugdale, later engraved (with significant changes) in his *Antiquities of Warwickshire* (1656). The idea was picked up in a double issue of the *Times Literary Supplement*, August 18 and 25, by Brian Vickers, who points out correctly that in the drawing as in the engraving 'The subject looks elderly, with a gaunt face and a drooping moustache', claiming also that 'he is shown with arms akimbo, resting his hands on a woolsack.' There is dispute about whether the alleged woolsack, in both the drawing and the monument as it exists, is really that, or rather some kind of writing cushion. John Shakespeare did deal in wool, but only as a sideline, and sometimes, at least, illegally. He better deserved commemoration for his services as alderman and bailiff.

Is it true?

Dugdale is known to have been careless in his representation of figures; his prime interest was in the recording of heraldic devices. Vickers dismisses evidence of this in his wish to believe that the drawing accurately represents the state of the bust in 1634.

It is not easy to discern exactly what Vickers (who, incidentally, erroneously refers to Henry Wriothesley, third Earl of Southampton, as the 'father of Shakespeare's patron') thinks may have happened. He admits that 'Some form of tribute to William Shakespeare' must have existed by 1623 when 'thy Stratford monument' is mentioned in lines by Leonard Digges printed in the First Folio. He supposes that 'some admirer(s), near or distant . . . celebrated the poet by adding a memorial to an existing family monument, near his grave under the chancel floor, rather than commissioning a new one.' The idea that the drawing represents a hybrid is presumably necessitated by the fact that, whether or not the person represented is Shakespeare's father, it clearly incorporates the lines in both Latin and English commemorating his son. Incorporation of the lines means that, if Vickers is right, the representation of the son as known to later ages must have been added, or substituted for that representing the father, after Dugdale made his drawing, in 1634, even though the lines praising the son were already in place. In a convoluted argument, Vickers proposes that whoever carved the monument in a state approximating to that in which it survives today 'worked from the previous monument.' I take this to mean that he believes the original bust to have been substantially modified so that it represented the son, not the father. He produces no evidence that the modification was a practical possibility.

It is known that the monument was repaired in 1749, and Vickers brushes aside specific contemporary statements that in the process it was not materially altered, in his claim that the monument as it exists at present differs greatly from that which it became in the later seventeenth century. I don't understand in what way, if any, this is relevant to his argument that it originally represented John Shakespeare, since he supposes it was materially altered in the early seventeenth century in any case.

VERDICT

Not true

HE DIED AS THE RESULT OF A DRINKING BOUT

WHO SAYS SO?

This story originates with the Rev. John Ward, a physician and clergyman who became vicar of Stratford in 1662, when Shakespeare's daughter Judith was still alive (she died later that year at the age of seventy-seven.) Unfortunately he didn't get round to talking to her. He records in his notebooks that 'Shakespeare, Drayton, and Ben Jonson had a merry meeting, and it seems drank too hard, for Shakespeare died of a fever there contracted.'

IS IT TRUE?

Ward seems an honest witness who took pains to record facts; Jonson was certainly a heavy drinker, though there is no other record of his visiting Stratford. Drayton however was a Warwickshire man and a frequent visitor to Clifford Chambers, very close to Stratford, who in later life was treated by Shakespeare's son-in-law, John Hall. There may be at least a grain of truth in it.

VERDICT

Possible

HE DIED OF SYPHILIS

WHO SAYS SO?

The most outspoken proponent of this theory is Katherine Duncan-Jones, in her book *Ungentle Shakespeare: Scenes from a Life* (2001). She writes that 'disturbingly graphic images of sweating tubs and venereal infection close both *Troilus and Cressida* and *Shakespeare's Sonnets*. Taken in conjunction with repeated gestures of retrospection and valediction in the late work, these images seem to me to support a supposition that Shakespeare's visits to Turnbull Street' — where his collaborator on *Pericles*, George Wilkins, kept an inn that doubled as a brothel — 'had left him with an unwanted legacy of infection, or at the very least, that he may have believed that they had done so. Again, it makes very little difference whether, from about 1608, he was indeed venereally infected, or whether he merely thought he was' (one might assume it made a lot of difference to him.) Writing that 'The treatment for syphilis was as much to be feared as the disease itself', she reproduces a fearsome engraving of an almost naked man in a sweating-tub, in which patients were treated with mercury. (*Pp. 224-5*) Earlier in the book she had written of 'the precise nature of Shakespeare's final illness', 'my own guess is that heart and circulatory trouble were added to latent syphilitic infection.' (*P. 266*) Duncan-Jones's speculations form the basis of scenes in William Boyd's television film 'A Waste of Shame: The Mystery of Shakespeare and his Sonnets' (on which Duncan-Jones acted as literary adviser, and in which she can be briefly glimpsed in a scene set at Thomas Thorpe's bookstall.)

IS IT TRUE?

The evidence is shaky. A writer does not need to have personal experience of his subject matter; the 'visits to Turnbull Street' are undocumented; and the sonnets printed at the end of the collection are the most derivative of all the poems, being based on Greek sources; nor are they as clearly concerned with venereal disease as Duncan-Jones implies.

VERDICT

Highly speculative

HE DIED OF TYPHOID FEVER

WHO SAYS SO?

This theory may lie behind the statement by the Rev. John Ward, vicar of Stratford-upon-Avon from 1662, that 'Shakespeare, Drayton, and Jonson had a merry meeting, and it seems drank too hard, for Shakespeare died of a fever there contracted.' *(See p. 83)* Much later, E. I. Fripp, a great authority on the Stratford records, building on Ward's report, wrote that 'Shakespeare proved, or became the victim of a malady, probably typhoid fever, which killed him.' Park Honan, in his biography (1998), remarking that Ward was a physician, gives credence to the theory. 'Typhoid', he writes, 'was virulent in a forward spring, and it is likely that Shakespeare's New Place was dangerous because of the fetid stream which ran down beside it to supply the fullers of cloth near the River Avon.' Furthermore, 'Shakespeare's illness lasted about as long as the normal time it takes for a typhoid victim to die.' (Pp. 406–7)

VERDICT

Possible – more likely than syphilis –, but not proven

He was murdered by his son-in-law, John Hall

In November 2005 the *Stratford-upon-Avon Herald* reported that a 'top team of American pathologists', led by James Starrs, Professor of Pathology at George Washington University, Washington D. C., were seeking permission to exhume Shakespeare's body in the hope of being able to demonstrate that he was murdered by his son-in-law, Dr John Hall. Starrs was reported also to have attempted autopsies on the bodies of 'the Boston strangler and Billy the Kid.'

What is the evidence?

No evidence was brought forward.

Arguments against.

John Hall was a highly respected physician. There is not the slightest reason to suppose that he would have murdered his father-in-law.

Verdict

Nonsense

THERE IS A DEATH MASK OF HIM

WHAT IS THE EVIDENCE?

In 1849 Ludwig Becker, a portrait painter from Darmstadt who had settled in Mainz, took to the British Museum in London a miniature oil painting which he had bought a few years previously. It had belonged to Count Francis von Kesselstadt, on whose death in 1841 the painting had been sold to the antique dealer from whom Becker bought it. It showed a corpse crowned with a laurel wreath – traditional tribute to a dead poet – and lying in state. It bore the date 1637. Becker believed that it represented Shakespeare, though according to Schoenbaum and others, 'the likeness (especially the nose, the wreath, and the date), all point to Jonson, the laureate who died in 1637.' Becker managed to reconcile the date with his claim that the picture showed Shakespeare by proposing that it had been copied in that year – an obvious fudging of the evidence. He learned that Kesselstadt had also owned a plaster of Paris cast of a face, which he claimed he had tracked down and bought from a junk dealer. He believed that the cast showed the same person as the painting. Not everyone agreed, if only because the mask bears the date 1616 – the year of Shakespeare's death. It is possible that this date is a late addition.

A number of questions are raised by the mask. Was Becker telling the truth? How did it get to Germany? If it is Shakespeare's death mask, why is it not closer in appearance to the Droeshout engraving and the bust? How likely is it that a death mask would have been made of a man of Shakespeare's social status? Nevertheless many people were impressed by it and by the claims made for it. It eventually went back to the ducal museum in Darmstadt. A charming painting of 1857 by Henry Wallis showing 'The Sculptor of the Stratford Bust before the Finished Work', now in the collections of the Royal Shakespeare Theatre, shows a sculptor in his studio looking over the River Avon, with his children playing beside him and a view of Holy Trinity Church visible through the window, while an assistant holds the mask from which he has carved the likeness. The mask is also said to have provided the model for the head of Shakespeare on the late-nineteenth-century monument created by Lord Ronald Gower now to be seen in the Theatre gardens. But the art historian M. H. Spielmann, in an *Encyclopaedia Britannica* article of 1904, expressed disbelief. It was put up for sale in 1960, but remained in Darmstadt. Its cause was taken up in 1995 by Professor Hildegard Hammerschmidt-Hummel, who initiated forensic tests which claimed to demonstrate its authenticity. She describes all this exhaustively in *The True Face of William Shakespeare* (2006). She interprets an apparent blemish on the right eye of the mask as evidence that he suffered from eye cancer. Might it not just as well be a stray drop of plaster? She agrees that the miniature represents Jonson. It is however ignored by Jonson's biographers, presumably because of doubts about its date.

VERDICT

I am highly sceptical

HE WROTE HIS OWN EPITAPH

WHO SAYS SO?

The gravestone under which Shakespeare has long been believed
to lie – it bears no name – is inscribed with the words:

> Good friend, for Jesus' sake forbear
> To dig the dust enclosèd here.
> Blest be the man that spares these stones,
> And curst be he that moves my bones.

This is probably designed to deter the sexton from moving the
bones after an interval into the charnel house that adjoined the
church. The nineteenth-century scholar James Orchard
Halliwell-Phillipps claimed to have found a similar epitaph on
a baker in a manuscript of about 1630:

> For Jesus Christ his sake forbear
> To dig the bones under this bier.
> Blessed is he who loves my dust,
> But damned be he who moves this crust.

The epitaph is first ascribed to Shakespeare in a manuscript of
about 1655-60. A letter from a lawyer, John Dowdall, who visited Stratford in 1693, also reports that Shakespeare made the
epitaph 'himself a little before his death.'

IS IT TRUE?

The anecdotal evidence is reasonably strong, but of course it is
just the sort of thing that would be said about a poet. The epitaph is written in the same metre as the epilogue to *The Tempest*,

which doesn't really prove much. Considered as poetry the lines are undistinguished.

Possible

HE DIED ON HIS BIRTHDAY

The monument in Holy Trinity Church, Stratford-upon-Avon is inscribed with the words: 'OBIIT A [N]NO DO[mini] 1616 Aetatis. 53 Die 23 Apr.' This means 'he died in the year 1616 at the age of 53 on 23 April.' As I say on p. 20, he was baptised on 26 April but the exact date of his birth is not known. As he was born in 1564, if he was 53 on 23 April 1616 he must have been born on or before that date.

VERDICT

Not known, but perfectly possible

Part two:

THE WRITINGS

❖

Is it true that…?

HE WROTE A POEM CALLED
'A Funeral Elegy'

WHAT IS IT?

A 578-line poem in iambic pentameters called 'A Funeral Elegy: in memory of the late virtuous Master William Peter of Whipton near Exeter' was published in 1612 by Thomas Thorpe, who three years previously had published Shakespeare's sonnets. Both the title page and dedication say that the poem was written by 'W. S.' Peter was a Devonshire gentleman born in 1582 and educated at Oxford. He married in 1609, had two daughters, and was stabbed to death on 15 January 1612 in a dispute over a horse after a hard day's drinking. The elegy appears to have been privately printed in an edition intended for the dead man's family and friends. Only two copies are known, both in Oxford. The poem attracted little attention until the publication in 1989 of *Elegy by W. S.: A Study in Attribution* by Donald Foster. Admitting that there are around 50 published authors of prose and verse of the period with the initials W. S., he nevertheless concluded that the poem's author was either William Strachey, known mainly as the writer of an account of a voyage to Virginia on which Shakespeare drew for *The Tempest*, or Shakespeare himself. In 1996 Foster and other scholars came out firmly in favour of Shakespeare's authorship. Much scholarly controversy ensued, but the poem was printed in three American editions of the Complete Works. In 2002 however the French scholar Gilles Monsarrat published an article attributing the poem to the dramatist

John Ford, and Foster and his followers accepted this attribution.

VERDICT

No

HE WROTE A POEM CALLED *Shall I die?*

IS THERE SUCH A POEM?

Yes, there are two early manuscripts of it, one in the Bodleian Library, Oxford, the other in Yale University Library.

WHAT'S IT LIKE?

It's an intricately rhyming love poem and has nine stanzas of ten lines each. Here's the first:

> Shall I die? Shall I fly
> Lovers' baits and deceits,
>   sorrow breeding?
> Shall I tend? Shall I send?
> Shall I sue, and not rue
>   my proceeding?
>   In all duty her beauty
> Binds me her servant for ever,
>   If she scorn, I mourn,
>   I retire to despair, joining never.

This intricate form of verse has not been found elsewhere in the period, but it closely resembles Robin Goodfellow's (Puck's) lines spoken over the sleeping Lysander in *A Midsummer Night's Dream*, 3.2.36-46.

WHO SAYS HE WROTE IT?

His name is written in full underneath the Oxford version, which probably dates from the late 1630s. It was first taken seriously in 1985 by Gary Taylor, working on the Oxford edition of the Complete Works. It provoked intense, world-wide publicity, much of it hostile, and some commentators have gone almost hysterical about its inclusion in the edition, even though there is no clear proof that Shakespeare didn't write it, and though most current editions include poems first printed in *The Passionate Pilgrim* in 1599 which are definitely not by Shakespeare, and though three of them print *A Funeral Elegy*, now known to be by John Ford *(see p. 95)*.

VERDICT

Perfectly possible

HE WROTE A PLAY CALLED
Edmond Ironside

WHAT IS IT?

Based mainly on Holinshed's *Chronicles*, this play, subtitled 'A True Chronicle History called *War Hath Made All Friends*' and set in the eleventh century, depicts battles between Edmund Ironside and King Canute. Written probably during the early 1590s, it survives only in an anonymous manuscript preserved in the British Library. It was first ascribed to Shakespeare by E. B. Everitt in *The Young Shakespeare* (1954). The claim was taken up by Eric Sams, who published an edition under the title of *Shakespeare's Lost Play* in 1986.

WHAT IS THE EVIDENCE?

The claims for Shakespeare's authorship rest mainly on linguistic grounds – correspondence of language and imagery with certain early plays of Shakespeare – along with the idea that the manuscript is in his handwriting.

IS IT TRUE?

Errors in the manuscript show pretty certainly that it is written by a scribe transcribing someone else's work, which invalidates any evidence adduced from handwriting. The linguistic evidence is shaky, and the play has not won acceptance in the canon.

VERDICT

Not true

HE WROTE A PLAY CALLED *Cardenio*

WHAT IS THE EVIDENCE?

On 9 September 1653 the London publisher Humphrey Moseley registered his intention to publish a batch of plays including 'The History of Cardenio, by Mr Fletcher and Shakespeare.' The title character figures in Cervantes's novel *Don Quixote*, which was published in an English version in 1612, around the time that Shakespeare was collaborating with Fletcher on *Henry VIII* and *The Two Noble Kinsmen*. On 20 May 1613 Shakespeare's company, the King's Men, were paid for a performance at court of six plays, including one called *Cardenno*, and on 9 July of that year the company received payment for a court performance of a play listed as *Cardenna*. These are clearly variant spellings of the same name.

It is natural to ask why, if Shakespeare really did collaborate with Fletcher on this play, Heminges and Condell did not include it in the First Folio, of 1623. The most obvious explanation is that they preferred not to reprint plays on which they knew that Shakespeare had collaborated with another writer unless there was a special reason for doing so. They omitted *Pericles*, on which we believe that Shakespeare collaborated with George Wilkins, and *The Two Noble Kinsmen*, published in 1634 as by Shakespeare and Fletcher. The other principal collaborative plays are *Henry VIII*, pretty certainly written by Shakespeare and Fletcher, which they had reason to include in order to complete the sequence of history plays, and *Timon of Athens*, now believed to have been written with Thomas Middleton, which they at first intended to omit but included to fill a temporary gap caused by copyright problems with *Troilus and Cressida.*

Cardenio has a curious afterlife. In 1728 Lewis Theobald, who was later to edit Shakespeare's Complete Plays, printed a tragi-comedy based on the story of Cardenio called *Double Falsehood, or The Distressed Lovers,* which he claimed to have 'written and adapted' from one 'written originally by W. Shakespeare.' It seems likely that a manuscript of the play written by Shakespeare and Fletcher somehow came into Theobald's hands, that he adapted it to suit the taste of the times, and that it was subsequently lost. In 1770 a newspaper reported that it was 'treasured up in the Museum of Covent Garden Playhouse.' The theatre and its library went up in smoke in 1808, and *Cardenio* may well have perished with them.

VERDICT

Probably true

HE WROTE A PLAY CALLED
Love's Labour's Won

WHAT'S THE EVIDENCE?

There's a book by Francis Meres called *Palladis Tamia –
Wit's Treasury* – published in 1598 which lists twelve plays
by Shakespeare (thirteen if by *Henry IV* he means Parts One
and Two). One of them is '*Love's Labour's Won.*' No play of this
name survives. For a long time it was assumed that Meres
was referring to another of Shakespeare's comedies by an
alternative title. It might be applied to *The Taming of the Shrew*,
which Meres doesn't name but is believed to have been written
by 1598. In itself it could refer to *All's Well that Ends Well*, but
that play is not believed to have been written by 1598. But in
1953 a fragment of a bookseller's list of around 1603 turned
up which includes *Love's Labour's Won* along with *The Merchant of
Venice, The Taming of a* [sic] *Shrew* and *Love's Labour's Lost*. No
author is named for any of them. On the basis of these two references it looks as if a play by Shakespeare called *Love's Labour's
Won* was in existence by 1598, that it had reached print by
around 1603, and that it was not included in the First Folio of
1623.

Many plays of the period were never printed, including *Cardenio*,
written partly by Shakespeare (*see p. 100*). The idea that a printed play may have been read out of existence is not impossible:
the first edition of *Titus Andronicus* was unknown until a copy
turned up in 1904 (but it had been reprinted in 1600 and
1611). At least two plays in which Shakespeare had a hand –

Pericles and *The Two Noble Kinsmen* — were omitted from the First Folio, and so was the lost *Cardenio*.

IS IT TRUE?

It seems likely to be true, but the play's absence from the Folio suggests that it may have been collaborative.

VERDICT

Probably true

HE WROTE PLAYS CALLED
The London Prodigal AND *A Yorkshire Tragedy*

WHAT ARE THEY?

These are two plays both of which were published in Shakespeare's lifetime with clear statements that he had written them. *The London Prodigal*, a lively city comedy with links to the biblical tale of the Prodigal Son, appeared in print in 1605 with the title page claim 'As it was played by the King's Majesty's servants. By William Shakespeare.' *A Yorkshire Tragedy* is a brief play – only about 700 lines long – which was registered for publication on 2 May 1608 as having been written by 'William Shakespeare.' It was reprinted in 1619 by the publisher Thomas Pavier along with a collection of Shakespearian and pseudo-Shakespearian texts. It is a powerful domestic drama which has had a number of successful productions and is available in several editions.

IS IT TRUE?

It would be difficult to deny the external evidence for Shakespeare's authorship were it not for the fact that neither play was included in the First Folio, of 1623, which appears to indicate that the compilers of that volume did not accept the attribution to Shakespeare. Both plays, however, were among the seven added to the third edition of the Folio, in 1664, only one of which – *Pericles* – is now accepted as having been written at least partly by Shakespeare and which have frequently been reprinted as apocryphal plays. Thomas Middleton, Thomas

Dekker and George Wilkins have all been suggested as author of *The London Prodigal*, but no agreement has been reached and it is best regarded as an anonymous work. Shakespeare's authorship of *A Yorkshire Tragedy* has had a few supporters, but the general scholarly view is that it was written by Thomas Middleton, and it is to be included in a collected edition of his complete works.

VERDICT

Almost certainly not true

HE WROTE PLAYS CALLED
Vortigern AND *Henry II*

WHAT ARE THEY?

William Henry Ireland (1775-1835) was the son of Samuel Ireland, a talented engraver and collector of books, pictures, and curiosities. The young man was fascinated by the life of Thomas Chatterton, 'the marvellous boy' who forged many pseudo-medieval poetical and other documents before dying of poisoning – his death was probably accidental but is often regarded as suicide – at the age of seventeen. On a visit to Stratford in or about 1794 father and son heard from John Jordan a cock and bull story about the alleged destruction a couple of weeks earlier of basketfuls of Shakespeare manuscripts to make room for a bevy of young partridges. This incident may have prompted William Henry to assuage his father's disappointment at the loss of such valuable relics by filling the gap himself. In the lawyer's office where he was employed he had access to spare leaves of parchment and old paper, and to ancient seals. Before long he proudly presented to his astonished and grateful father a stream of papers including business documents about the Globe, letters to Shakespeare from Queen Elizabeth and the Earl of Southampton, a love letter accompanied by a lock of hair and verses written by William Shakespeare to 'Anne Hatherreweaye', appendices to Shakespeare's will making amends for the implied slight in the bequest to Anne of the 'second-best bed', a new manuscript of *King Lear* improved by the omission of bawdy passages and obscurities, manuscript extracts from *Hamlet*, and a new portrait of Shakespeare (see

Frontispiece.) He tried to deflect scepticism about the portrait by forging a letter in which Shakespeare described it as 'a whymsycalle conceyte'. Later he offered his father two previously unknown plays by Shakespeare, *Vortigern* and *Henry II*, explaining that they had all come from a chest in the house of a friend who preferred to remain anonymous. Samuel invited literary friends to inspect the finds. Among those who paid homage was James Boswell, who fell to his knees, kissed the relics, and declared that he could now die happy. He did, three months later. Controversy raged; there were many sceptics, including the scholar Edmond Malone. It must seem astonishing that anyone who knew Shakespeare's writings could have believed him capable of addressing to his beloved – or to anyone else – such twaddle as

> Is there inne heavenne aught more rare
> Thanne thou sweete nymphe of Avon fayre
> Is there onne Earthe a Manne more trewe
> Thanne Willy Shakspeare is toe you.

Nevertheless, authorities from the College of Heralds proclaimed the relics authentic. Samuel published an impressive volume of facsimiles and transcripts but before long Malone savaged the enterprise in a 400-page volume called *An Inquiry into the Authenticity of Certain Miscellaneous Papers and Legal Instruments*.... The death blow came three days after Malone's book was published, when the actor and theatre manager John Philip Kemble put on a performance of *Vortigern* at Drury Lane which is one of the all-time great disasters of theatre history. The play's banal language caused titters during the first part of the performance, and the death blow came towards the end when Kemble had to say 'And when this solemn mockery is over.' The audience howled with laughter and the play came to an abrupt end. Eventually William Henry admitted his fraud, but his loyal father continued to proclaim his son's innocence, publishing the new plays in 1799 and even trying to have *Henry II* performed.

VERDICT

Not true

HE HELPED TO TRANSLATE THE
AUTHORIZED VERSION OF THE BIBLE

There is a story, 'Proofs of Holy Writ', by Rudyard Kipling in which he imagines Shakespeare and Ben Jonson conversing in Shakespeare's Stratford garden when they receive a missive from Miles Smith, known to have been one of the translators of the King James Version of the Bible, asking for help with translating part of the Book of Isaiah. They talk it over, Shakespeare benefiting from Jonson's classical learning, make comparisons with earlier translations, and produce an improved version which they send to Smith. They are aware that no one is likely ever to know that they made their contribution:

> 'Who will know we had part in it?' Ben asked.
> 'God, maybe—if He ever lay ear to earth,' replies Shakespeare.

There is an independent story which is sometimes used in support of the theory while not exactly saying that Shakespeare was a translator. So far as I know it originates in a letter to *The Times* in 1976 from Bishop Mark Hudson. He wrote: 'If you look up Psalm 46 in the Authorized Version of the Bible and count 46 words from the beginning of the psalm, you will find that you have arrived at the word "shakes". Now, discounting the word "Selah", count 46 words from the end of the psalm and the word then revealed is "spear." This astonishing cryptogram is virtually unknown. Psalm 46, 46th word from the beginning, 46th word from the end: "Shakespeare"'. He finds this especially remarkable because the Authorized Version was published in 1610, in which year Shakespeare was 46 years old. In fact he goes so far as to propose that 'To honour Shakespeare on his birthday, the translator placed this cipher in Psalm 46, 46th word from the beginning, 46th word from the end.'

Is it true?

The cheating in the Bishop's claim is evident in the requirement that in counting the words, one of them should be omitted. Moreover the names of the 47 or so scholars and clergymen who translated, or revised, the Bible are known, and Shakespeare's is not among them.

Verdict

Pure fiction

A Midsummer Night's Dream WAS WRITTEN TO CELEBRATE A WEDDING

WHO SAYS SO?

This supposition originated with Ludwig Tieck, the German poet and translator who produced the play in 1843, with an overture and incidental music specially composed by Felix Mendelssohn. In 1830 Tieck had suggested that the 'germ or first sketch' of the play was a masque-like compliment to Shakespeare's friend and patron the Earl of Southampton on his marriage to Elizabeth Vernon in 1598, the year in which the play is first mentioned in print. He produced no evidence. Since then the theory has been often repeated and elaborated, and a wide variety of aristocratic weddings – at least eleven of them – have been identified as the putative occasion for the play.

WHAT IS THE EVIDENCE?

There is no documentary evidence to support the theory. It relies mainly on the fact that the play is much concerned with love and marriage, and especially that it ends in the marriage of three pairs of lovers – Theseus and Hippolyta, Hermia and Lysander, and Helena and Demetrius – whose nuptials are blessed by the newly reconciled Fairy King and Queen, Oberon and Titania. In addition the play contains at least one possible compliment to Queen Elizabeth, who might have been present at an aristocratic wedding, and it needs the services of a larger number of singing boy actors than usual.

What are the Arguments Against It?

One is the absence of documentary evidence. This is just the kind of event that would have been recorded in aristocratic families, if only among accounts for payments to the performers. Another is the absence of any other record of a play of this nature having been written for a private function in Shakespeare's time. Yet another is the fact that the play was certainly performed in public theatres. Moreover a great many other plays of the period are also concerned with love and marriage.

Verdict

Unlikely

Sir John Falstaff was first called Sir John Oldcastle

What is the evidence?

We know from various pieces of evidence that the character in *Henry the Fourth* Part One named Sir John Falstaff was originally named after his historical counterpart, the Protestant martyr Sir John Oldcastle. A pun on his name survives in the opening scene, where the Prince calls him 'my old lad of the castle.' Moreover the epilogue to this play's sequel, *Henry the Fourth* Part Two, ends with 'If you be not too much cloyed with fat meat, our humble author will continue the story with Sir John in it, and make you merry with fair Catherine of France; where, for anything I know, Falstaff shall die of a sweat – unless already a be killed with your hard opinions. For Oldcastle died a martyr, and this is not the man.' It seems clear that Shakespeare changed the character's surname because of protests from his descendants, the influential Cobham family, one of whom – William Brooke, seventh Lord Cobham – was Queen Elizabeth's Lord Chamberlain, responsible for court entertainments, from August 1596 until his death on 5 March 1597 – that is, around the time the play first appeared. The name Oldcastle was restored in Part One in the Oxford edition of 1986, to howls of protest from traditionalists.

Verdict

True

HE WROTE *The Merry Wives of Windsor* IN TWO WEEKS AT THE REQUEST OF QUEEN ELIZABETH, WHO HAD ASKED FOR A PLAY ABOUT 'SIR JOHN IN LOVE.'

WHAT IS THE EVIDENCE?

This idea goes back to 1702. The dramatist John Dennis wrote an adaptation of *The Merry Wives of Windsor* called *The Comical Gallant: or The Amours of Sir John Falstaff*. In the Preface he said that the original play 'pleased one of the greatest queens that ever was in the world. .... This comedy was written at her command, and by her direction, and she was so eager to see it acted that she commanded it to be finished in fourteen days.' Two years later he reduced the time of composition to ten days. The story was picked up and elaborated by Nicholas Rowe in 1709, in his short biography of Shakespeare which accompanied his edition of the Complete Works, where he wrote that the Queen 'was so well pleased with that admirable character of Falstaff in the two Parts of *Henry the Fourth* that she commanded him to continue in it for one play more, and to show him in love.' Then in the following year Charles Gildon embroidered the tale even more: 'The fairies in the fifth act makes a handsome compliment to the Queen in her palace of Windsor, who had obliged him to write a play of Sir John Falstaff in love, and which I am very well assured he performed in a fortnight; a prodigious thing, when all is so well contrived, and carried on without the least confusion.' It looks as if Rowe and Gildon were simply embroidering what Dennis had written, and Dennis may have invented the tale. It is certainly true however that the play contains compliments to the Queen as well as a long passage about Windsor Castle, which would make it plausible that it was written (or perhaps adapted) for performance there before the Queen.

IS IT TRUE?

There may be a grain of truth in it

HE PORTRAYED HIMSELF AS HAMLET

Many readers have fancied that real-life characters are portrayed, with varying degrees of realism, in the plays. Naturally enough, Shakespeare himself has been most readily found in particularly intelligent characters, among whom Hamlet is preeminent. Another is Biron in *Love's Labour's Lost*. I suppose that any dramatist draws upon aspects of his own personality in portraying other people, and it is not unreasonable to imagine that some characters in Shakespeare's plays bear a higher degree of resemblance to their creator than others. On the other hand there is no way in which Hamlet can be regarded as a self-portrait in any normal sense of the word.

VERDICT

Not really

THE DEATH OF OPHELIA IN *Hamlet* IS BASED ON A REAL-LIFE INCIDENT.

WHAT IS THE EVIDENCE?

On 17 December 1579, when Shakespeare was fifteen, Katherine Hamlett, an unmarried woman of unknown age, drowned in the River Avon. At the inquest held on 11 February 1580, the coroner's jury concluded that 'going with a milk pail to draw water at the River Avon, standing on the bank of the same', she 'suddenly and by accident, slipped and fell into the river, and was drowned; and met her death in no other wise or fashion.' Edgar I. Fripp, in *Shakespeare: Man and Artist* (1938), speculated that in fact she committed suicide, thus giving Shakespeare the idea for Ophelia's drowning: 'All this throws light on the story of Ophelia, which, we can hardly doubt, was fashioned out of the Poet's youthful recollection of the drowning of Katharine Hamlet in the Avon.' (Vol. I, p. 147) Fripp was encouraged in his belief by the supposition that Shakespeare was working in a Stratford lawyer's office at the time, and so would have had first-hand knowledge of the inquest. The idea is taken up by other writers including Katherine Duncan-Jones, in *Ungentle Shakespeare* (2001), pp. 152-3 .

VERDICT

'an intriguing speculation, no more' (Schoenbaum, p. 501)

Troilus and Cressida WAS NOT PERFORMED IN ENGLAND UNTIL THE TWENTIETH CENTURY

WHAT IS THE EVIDENCE?

When this play was first printed, in 1609, it had two variant title pages. One of them says that it had been 'acted by the King's Majesty's servants at the Globe.' The other, however, omits this claim and says in its preface that it had never been 'staled with the stage, never clapper-clawed with the palms of the vulgar.' No satisfactory resolution to these apparently conflicting statements has ever been made. There is however no other reference to its having been acted in its own time. A heavily adapted version by John Dryden called *All for Love, or the World Well Lost*, first staged in 1677, was acted from time to time over the next half century, but the first record of a performance of Shakespeare's play is in a burlesque version acted by an all-male cast in Munich in 1898. William Poel directed a semi-professional production in London and Stratford in 1912-1913, memorable mainly for the first appearance as an actress of Edith Evans. Effectively however it owes its current reputation largely to amateur performances by the Marlowe Society of Cambridge directed by George Rylands in 1928 and later.

VERDICT

Could easily be true

Macbeth IS AN UNLUCKY PLAY

This theatrical superstition goes back a long way. Many actors regularly refuse to quote from or to name the play, referring to it instead as 'The Scottish Play.' It is the partial subject of a book, *The Curse of Macbeth: with other Theatrical Superstitions and Ghosts* (1981), by Richard Huggett. Like many others, Huggett repeats a legend that the play was first presented at Hampton Court, and that at this performance the boy actor Hal Berridge, playing Lady Macbeth, 'was suddenly taken ill with a fever, and at such short notice that the only possible substitute was the author himself.' To the best of my belief however every detail of this story, including the place of performance and the name of the actor, along with an equally picturesque account of a performance allegedly written by Samuel Pepys, was invented and attributed to John Aubrey by that supreme ironist Max Beerbohm in a review of a performance by Johnstone Forbes-Robertson and Mrs Patrick Campbell printed in the *Saturday Review* on 1 October 1898.

Huggett — not an entirely reliable guide — accumulates a number of tales of disaster associated with performances of the play, such as the statement that during an Old Vic production of 1954 'there were two abortions and an attempted suicide in the company, the company manager broke both his legs in a car accident and an electrician in Dublin electrocuted himself causing first-class burns, and amongst the physical accidents in the fights were several broken legs and a nearly-gouged eye.' Furthermore, he alleges, when the production toured in South Africa a passer-by watching the scenery being unloaded 'enquired which play was to be performed. "Macbeth", said one of the stage hands and the minute he said it, a spear which was being craned up and poised high in the air with a bundle of others, dislodged itself and fell right on the stranger's head, killing him instantly.'

It is certainly true that many eminent actors, most notoriously Peter O'Toole at the Old Vic in 1980, have failed in the central role, though this may be rather because of the way the play is written than the result of supernatural influences.

IS IT TRUE?

Yes, if you believe it

He portrayed himself as Prospero in *The Tempest*

Who says so?

The idea seems to derive from the Preface written by Thomas Campbell to an edition of Shakespeare of 1838. In it he writes:

> Shakspeare, as if conscious that it would be his last, and as if inspired to typify himself, has made its hero a natural, a dignified, and benevolent magician, who could conjure up spirits from the vasty deep, and command supernatural agency by the most seemingly natural and simple means. Here Shakspeare himself is Prospero, or rather the superior genius who commands both Prospero and Ariel.

Is it true?

Of course Prospero is in no literal sense a self-portrait. On the other hand some of his functions in the play, such as father, artist, and surrogate playwright, link him with his creator. It is sometimes suggested that Prospero's insistence that his daughter, Miranda, retain her virginity until she marries may reflect Shakespeare's concern about his own daughters, and may even reveal incestuous feelings for one or both of them.

Verdict

Not really

HE BORROWED MUCH OF HIS LANGUAGE

The language of the books that Shakespeare drew on for his stories often shows through his actual telling of them. In other words, at times he incorporates words and phrases from the books that must have lain open before him as he wrote into the dialogue that his characters speak. This is especially liable to happen when he is at his least inspired, giving information necessary for the plot. Look for example at this extract from *Henry V*:

> Hugh Capet also – who usurped the crown
> Of Charles the Duke of Lorraine, sole heir male
> Of the true line and stock of Charles the Great –
> To fine his title with some shows of truth,
> Though in pure truth it was corrupt and naught,
> Conveyed himself as heir to th'Lady Lingard,
> Daughter to Charlemain, who was the son
> To Louis the Emperor, and Louis the son
> Of Charles the Great (1.2.69-77)

Now compare the words I have underlined there to the following passage from Shakespeare's main source for the play, Holinshed's *Chronicles*:

> Hugh Capet also, who usurped the crown upon Charles Duke of Lorraine, the sole male heir of the line and stock of Charles the Great, to make his title seem true and appear good, though indeed it was stark naught, conveyed himself as heir to the Lady Lingard, daughter to King Charlemagne, son to Louis the Emperor, that was son to Charles the Great.

In that passage – admittedly an extreme example – Shakespeare is doing little more than versify the prose of his source.

There are other passages, however, where although he draws quite heavily on his original, he transmutes good prose into great poetry. An example is Enobarbus's famous description of Cleopatra in 'The barge she sat in' (*Antony and Cleopatra*, 2.2.199-221), where Shakespeare is indebted to Sir Thomas North's translation of Plutarch. Another example of the same sort of thing is to be found in *The Tempest*, where Prospero's great speech beginning 'Ye elves of hills, brooks, standing lakes and groves' (5.1.33-57) closely paraphrases a speech from Arthur Golding's translation of Ovid's *Metamorphoses*.

VERDICT

There is some truth in it

He borrowed most of his plots

Who says so?

This is a frequently stated comment deriving from the fact that most of Shakespeare's plays (like those of most of his contemporaries) derive from pre-existing stories, many of them historical such as *Julius Caesar, Coriolanus, Antony and Cleopatra* and the plays about English history, others fictional, such as *The Merchant of Venice, Othello,* and *The Winter's Tale.* Bernard Shaw praised his 'gift of telling a story (provided someone else told it to him first.)' There are only a few plays, including *Love's Labour's Lost, A Midsummer Night's Dream,* and *The Tempest,* which make little or no use of stories that had already been told. But it is necessary to make a distinction between narrative material and dramatic plots. In all the plays in which Shakespeare uses pre-existing material he rearranges the order of events and the time schemes, adds characters, invents additional episodes, and generally turns stories into drama.

Verdict

Not really true

HE USES AN EXCEPTIONALLY LARGE VOCABULARY

Shakespeare was writing at a time when the English language was in an unusual state of flux. Many English books, and even plays (though not those intended for the popular theatre) were still written wholly in Latin, because this was the best way to achieve an international readership. Shakespeare himself uses many Latin tags and quotations, especially in his earlier plays, such as *Titus Andronicus*. The English language was struggling to achieve a vocabulary and expressive power comparable to that offered by Latin. This process involved much coining of new words, often on the basis of, especially, Latin and French. It also encouraged the use of old words in new forms, senses and combinations. Shakespeare was certainly an innovator, as his contemporaries were aware. Francis Meres, in a book published in 1598, praised him as one by whom 'The English tongue is mightily enriched, and gorgeously invested in rare ornaments and resplendent habiliments.'

Shakespeare's works contain around 900,000 words. It has been calculated that his active vocabulary as revealed by his works was made up of between 20,000 and 30,000 words – it is impossible to be precise both because of the difficulty of defining exactly what we mean by a word – do compounds, negative forms, names, and deliberate mistakes count, for instance? – and because of variants between the texts. Some scholars would put the total lower than this – Professor David Crystal estimates it at between 17,000 and 20,000, which he says 'is quite small by modern standards, though probably much larger than his contemporaries.' And the same scholar estimates that 'the number of his lexical innovations, insofar as these can be identified reliably, are [sic] probably no more than 1,700, less than half of which have remained in the language.' This is not enormous; on the other hand Crystal admits that 'no other author matches these impressive figures.' Some words apparently coined by Shakespeare are still in use: examples are abstemious, accommodation, addiction, comply, discontent, frugal, and reinforcement. Many others are no longer current – examples are comart, cursorary, empiricutic, exsufflicate, incony, questrist, and villagery, all unknown to my spell checker. He was especially fond of coining negative forms beginning with –un, such as unprofited, untender, untitled, and untutored.

VERDICT

True

THE SONNETS

❖

MR W. H. IS WILLIAM HATHAWAY

The dedication to *Shakespeare's Sonnets* of 1609, signed with the initials T. T. – i.e. Thomas Thorpe, who published the volume – refers to 'the only begetter of these ensuing sonnets, Mr W. H.' 'Only begetter' is open to a variety of interpretations. It is usually assumed to refer to the person who inspired them (although in fact it is clear that at the very least two different persons, one male and one female, are addressed.) Alternatively it could mean the person who procured them for publication. In 1986 the critic and scholar Barbara Everett, of Somerville College Oxford, published an article called 'Mrs Shakespeare' in the *London Review of Books* suggesting that the carrier was Anne Shakespeare's brother William Hathaway. She writes: 'Conceivable as a powerful, even attractively masculine woman, eight years older than the writer; one capable of obsessing her young husband for many miserable jealous years, then of maddening and amusing and at last ("second-best bed") boring him – it is believable that this perhaps ambitious, clever and wilful woman impatiently sent her brother off to London with the bundle of fair-copied, brilliant, confused poems which her obstinate husband wouldn't publish and which she in any case remembered, rightly or wrongly, as being mostly addressed to herself and therefore arguably her own.' A. L. Rowse's reaction was 'Rubbish! Absolute rot! ... Is there no end to human foolery?'

Is it true?

Everett's remarks on Anne make unprovable assumptions about her character and her relationship with her husband. The idea that she would be anxious to see in print love poems which are manifestly not addressed to herself, many of which are extremely unflattering, seems improbable.

Verdict

Guesswork

THE FIRST SEVENTEEN SONNETS WERE COMMISSIONED BY A MOTHER WHO WANTED HER SON TO MARRY

IS IT TRUE?

These poems certainly exhort their addressee to marry and beget a child, or more specifically a son. Sonnet 3 includes the lines 'Thou art thy mother's glass, and she in thee / Calls back the lovely April of her prime', but there is no specific evidence that any of them were written to commission. Moreover the intimate tone of some of them implies that the poet was already close to the person they address.

VERDICT

Not true

Sonnet 145 from the 1609 volume of Shakespeare's sonnets reads as follows:

> Those lips that Love's own hand did make
>> Breathed forth the sound that said I hate
> To me that languished for her sake:
>> But when she saw my woeful state,
> Straight in her heart did mercy come,
>> Chiding that tongue that ever sweet
> Was used in giving gentle doom,
>> And taught it thus anew to greet:
> 'I hate' she altered with an end
>> That followed it as gentle day
> Doth follow night, who like a fiend
>> From heaven to hell is flown away.
> 'I hate' from hate away she threw,
> And saved my life, saying 'not you.'

It is unusual in its form, being written, unlike most of the Sonnets, in eight-syllabled lines (octosyllabics, or tetrameters), instead of the standard ten-syllabled lines (iambic pentameters). It is also a rather undistinguished poem, easily imagined as having been written early in its author's career. Most interestingly, the word play on 'hate' and 'hate away' can easily be read as a playful pun on the name Hath-away. From this Professor Andrew Gurr, as recently as 1971, deduced that it was written at the time Shakespeare was courting Anne, around 1582, when he was about eighteen, which would mean that it is almost certainly his earliest surviving composition.

VERDICT
Probably true

The first 126 sonnets are addressed to a young man

What is the evidence?

Some among the first 126 of the Sonnets as printed in 1609 are certainly addressed to a male, as we can see from forms of address – e.g. 'lovely boy' (Sonnet 126) – and pronouns. Moreover all those that are certainly addressed to a female – the so-called 'dark lady', a phrase that does not occur in these poems – are printed among the last 28. But many of the first 126 could be addressed to, or written about, either a male or a female. Many scholars, including some who should know better, write as if all these poems were addressed to a male, and, moreover, to the same person. In fact this idea is no more than a deduction based on context.

Verdict

Not true without serious qualification

ALL THE SONNETS ARE ADDRESSED TO QUEEN ELIZABETH

WHO SAYS SO?

In 1797 a lawyer and political writer named George Chalmers wrote a book called *An Apology for the Believers in the Shakespeare Papers*, followed two years later by a *Supplemental Apology*... These were contributions to a controversy over extensive Shakespeare forgeries perpetrated by a young man called William Henry Ireland, who forged innumerable alleged Shakespeare documents including two new plays, one of which was performed at Drury Lane. It was laughed off the stage. *(See p. 100)* But many eminent persons, including Chalmers, were taken in. The level of his literary intelligence may be judged by the fact that in these books he proposed that all Shakespeare's sonnets were addressed to Queen Elizabeth, explaining that she was often thought of as a man. His theory was designed in part to exonerate Shakespeare from having written love poems to a male object. He expressed himself astonished at the idea that 'Shakespeare, a husband, a father, a moral man, addressed a hundred and twenty, nay, a hundred and twenty six, *Amourous* Sonnets to a male object.' He experienced notable difficulty in explaining how Sonnet 20, with its bawdy puns on the word 'prick', might have been addressed to Her Majesty.

IS IT TRUE?

No

The 'Dark Lady' sonnets are addressed to Mary Fitton

Who says so?

This theory was expounded at a meeting of the New Shakspere Society in 1884, and two years later in an introduction to a facsimile edition of the sonnets, by a theological and literary scholar, Thomas Tyler. Mary Fitton was an aristocrat who became lady in waiting to Queen Elizabeth around 1598, and later the mistress of William Herbert, third Earl of Pembroke, by whom she had a son. The theory complemented the belief that Herbert was the 'Mr W. H.' of Thorpe's dedication to the sonnets (see p. 60). It was popular for a while, but dented by the discovery in 1897 of a portrait which showed that she was not all that dark. Bernard Shaw took it up, as a convenient fiction, in his playlet *The Dark Lady of the Sonnets*, of 1910, and it continued in circulation for some years.

Verdict

No more likely than any other of the candidates

The 'Dark Lady' Sonnets are
addressed to Emilia Lanier

Who says so?

In 1973 the historian A. L. Rowse published a book called *Shakespeare the Man* in which he declared that he had finally discovered the identity of the 'Dark Lady.' She was Emilia Lanier, born in 1569 into a family of court musicians named Bassano. Much of his evidence derived from the voluminous, little explored papers of the Elizabethan astrologer, magician and physician, Simon Forman. These revealed that Emilia was the mistress of the elderly Henry Carey, 1st Lord Hunsdon, patron of Shakespeare's company as the Lord Chamberlain's Men, and mother of his illegitimate son. After becoming pregnant in 1592 she was married to Captain Alphonse Lanier, member of another family of court musicians. Carey died in 1596.

Emilia was an interesting woman, a religious poet of talent, as she showed in a volume of poems called *Salve Deus Rex Judaeorum* but written in English, published in 1611. She died in 1645. Rowse's theory depended in part on Forman's description of her as having been, Rowse believed, 'brown in youth.' It happened that the BBC asked me to take part in a broadcast with Rowse at the time the book appeared. Glancing at the photo-facsimile of extracts from Forman's papers, I suspected that what Forman actually wrote was 'braue' – meaning fine, handsome – not 'brown', and a trip to the Bodleian Library convinced me that I was right. When I confronted Rowse with this during the broadcast he tried to bluster his way out of it, and he maintained this position for some time afterwards, while eventually withdrawing his claim.

The misreading 'brown' was Rowse's only evidence that Emilia was dark. In itself it does not disprove the theory, but all the evidence is circumstantial.

VERDICT

Not proven; and it is not even certain that the 'dark lady' ever really existed

The 'Dark Lady' sonnets are addressed to Mrs Florio

Who says so?

This idea was floated, if only half-seriously, by Jonathan Bate in his best-selling book *The Genius of Shakespeare* (1997). John Florio (1553-1625) was a distinguished literary scholar, translator and language teacher, son of an Italian refugee and his English wife. The Earl of Southampton, to whom Shakespeare dedicated his narrative poems, and the Earl of Pembroke, to whom the Folio was dedicated, were among his patrons, and Florio lived for a while in Southampton's household. Passages in some of Shakespeare's plays are based on writings by Florio, including his great translation of Montaigne's *Essays*, and Shakespeare is very likely to have known him. Florio's wife – whose first name is unknown, as is her colouring – was a sister of the poet Samuel Daniel. 'Unromantic as the thought may be,' writes Bate, 'there is no reason why we should not imagine Shakespeare sleeping with Florio's wife as well as pilfering his library and mocking his phrases.' But, he admits, 'we will never know whether Shakespeare and/or Southampton really slept with Florio's wife.'

Verdict

Not proven

The 'Dark Lady sonnets' are addressed to a woman who was black of skin

Who says so?

This theory has been traced back to a book by Wilhelm Jordan, *Shakespeares Gedichte* (1861), in which he asks 'whether the seductress whose breasts were dun (dark brown) and had wires (hence twisting, curling) was not a mulatto or quadroon from the West Indies, with African blood coursing through her veins, and the musical sense common to her rhythmic race'. It resurfaced, not entirely seriously, in G. B. Harrison's book *Shakespeare under Elizabeth* (1933), in which he notes that at revels held in Gray's Inn in the 1590s mock homage was paid to the prince of the revels by 'Lucy Negro, Abbess de Clerkenwell.' (Abbess is a satirical way of calling her a madam, head of a brothel.) Others followed, and the idea was more seriously pursued by Margreta de Grazia in an article called 'The Scandal of Shakespeare's Sonnets.'

Is it true?

There is no way of either proving or disproving this

THE SONNETS SHOW THAT ANOTHER POET IS SHAKESPEARE'S RIVAL FOR THE FAVOURS OF A YOUNG MAN

Some of the sonnets appear to refer to an unnamed poet who was a rival to the author's love. Sonnet 79 speaks of one who wielded 'a worthier pen' than the author, and is 'a better spirit' to whom the poet is 'inferior far.' Sonnet 86 speaks of 'the proud full sail' of his 'great verse' and conjectures that 'his spirit' was 'by spirits taught to write / Above a mortal pitch.' And he has a mysterious 'affable familiar ghost / Which nightly gulls him with intelligence.' Worst of all, the fair young man's 'countenance filled up' the rival's 'line', depriving the poet of 'matter.' This all provides scant grounds for identifying the rival. The playwright and poet George Chapman has been suggested because his often bombastic verse might be said to have a 'proud full sail.' Ben Jonson has also been nominated, and figures in this capacity in the television film 'A Waste of Shame' (p. 60), and so has Christopher Marlowe.

VERDICT

Probably true

AUTHORSHIP

❖

HE DIDN'T WRITE THE PLAYS ATTRIBUTED TO HIM

WHO SAID IT FIRST?

The idea goes back to about 1785, when a Warwickshire clergyman, James Wilmot, suggested that Francis Bacon was their author. It appears next in a book called, surprisingly, *The Romance of Yachting*, of 1848, by an American lawyer, Colonel Joseph C. Hart. It grew in force from the middle of the nineteenth century, since when at least 60 people – the number grows annually – have been proposed as the plays' author. I write about some of the more prominent candidates in later entries.

IS THERE ANY REASON TO BELIEVE IT?

No. There is a mass of evidence from Shakespeare's time that the plays and poems were written by a man called William Shakespeare. For instance:

There are printed references to him, by name, during his lifetime as a writer of poems and/or plays by authors including Henry Willobie (1594), William Covell (1595), Richard

Barnfield, Francis Meres (both 1598), John Weever (1599), the anonymous author of a play called *The Return from Parnassus* (printed in 1606 but written earlier), Henry Chettle (1603), Anthony Scoloker (1604), William Barksted (1607), John Webster (1612), and Thomas Freeman (1614). There are also of course numerous references in the years following his death. Among the most notable of these are references to him in intimate conversations around Christmas of 1618 between his friend, colleague and rival Ben Jonson and a Scottish poet named William Drummond in which Jonson spoke frankly, admiringly, but also somewhat critically of Shakespeare. Drummond made notes about these conversations which are very revealing about Shakespeare, Jonson, and many other writers of the time.

There are also allusions to Shakespeare by name as a writer in manuscripts written during his lifetime including one by Gabriel Harvey (about 1601) which refers to *The Rape of Lucrece* and *Hamlet*, by the anonymous author of a play called *The Pilgrimage to Parnassus* (c. 1598-1601), in financial accounts for plays performed before the royal family at court (1604-5), by Leonard Digges (c. 1613), and by the playwright Francis Beaumont (1613).

Shakespeare's name appears on the dedications and the title pages of the two long poems, *Venus and Adonis*, in 1593, and *The Rape of Lucrece*, in 1594 and on the title pages of many editions of his plays from 1598 onwards, and on reprints of the poems and the first edition of the Sonnets (1609).

Seven years after his death his collected plays were printed as his in the book known as the First Folio, which includes a number of tributes to him as well as an engraved portrait.

That the author of the plays was indeed the man from Stratford is shown especially by the two inscriptions on his memorial in Holy Trinity Church, Stratford, which compare him to great figures of antiquity and praise what 'he hath writ'; by the verses by Ben Jonson in the First Folio of 1623 which refer to him as the 'sweet swan of Avon'; and by the poem also in the Folio by Leonard Digges which refers to his 'Stratford monument.' It is also notable that a number of people visited Stratford in pilgrimage to his grave in the years following his death: as early as 1634 a Lieutenant Hammond recorded his visit to 'the neat monument of that famous English poet Mr William Shakespeare.'

VERDICT

Shakespeare wrote Shakespeare. A selection of the many attempts to show that he did not do so are discussed in the following pages. The important thing to remember is that before saying he could not have done so you need to disprove the evidence that he did. It's no use saying things like 'he couldn't have known enough', or 'he didn't travel enough', or 'he wasn't aristocratic enough' in face of the overwhelming evidence from his own time that a man called William Shakespeare who came from Stratford-upon-Avon wrote the plays and poems for which he is famous.

Reservation

Just to keep things straight, Shakespeare did not write all the plays single-handed. In some of them he worked with other writers, especially, towards the end of his career, John Fletcher.

And a few plays, notably one called *A Yorkshire Tragedy*, almost certainly by Thomas Middleton, and another called *The London Prodigal* (of unknown authorship) were wrongly said to have been by him in his own time *(see p. 104)*. This may have been a kind of advertising ploy, taking advantage of his fame.

He cannot have been well educated enough to have written the plays and poems.

Who says so?

This is often said by people wishing to argue that Shakespeare didn't write his works.

Is it true?

Stratford had a good grammar school. Its records don't survive so we have no list of its pupils. As the son of an alderman, Shakespeare would have been entitled to attend free. The Elizabethan educational system was excellent, at least for boys. After going to a petty school, where they learned to read and write, they started grammar school at the age of about seven, and normally stayed till they were about fifteen. The syllabus concentrated on classical literature and rhetoric. Pupils were taught Latin from the age of around seven upwards, and had to speak in Latin as soon as they could do so. Shakespeare shows a boy – called William – being quizzed about his Latin grammar by his teacher in *The Merry Wives of Windsor* (4.1). This is more clearly likely to be based directly on his own experience than any other scene in his plays, which show familiarity with exactly the kind of reading that would have been required in the grammar school.

A number of Stratford boys went to university. Shakespeare seems not to have done so – the records of the universities are preserved – but there is nothing in his plays or poems that could not have been written by a former grammar school boy who carried on reading after he left school.

VERDICT

Not true

CHRISTOPHER MARLOWE WROTE THE PLAYS

WHO SAID IT FIRST?

A novel of 1895 called *It Was Marlowe: A Story of Three Centuries*, by the American William Gleason Ziegler, has a Preface claiming that Marlowe died not, as was supposed, in 1593 but five years later, and that he wrote all Shakespeare's 'stronger plays'. That claim is particularly odd since most of what are normally regarded as 'the stronger plays' date from after 1598. Among many other writings taking up the theory is a mischievously entertaining novel, *History Play: The Lives and Afterlife of Christopher Marlowe* (2004), by Rodney Bolt.

WHO TOOK UP THE IDEA?

In 1955 the American journalist Calvin Hoffman published a book called *The Murder of the Man Who Was 'Shakespeare'* suggesting that Marlowe's supposed lover, Thomas Walsingham, faked Marlowe's death in 1593 and smuggled him abroad. Walsingham supposedly arranged for William Shakespeare to pose as the author of poems and plays actually written by Marlowe, who returned to live in obscurity in England. Hoffman left his estate to the King's School Canterbury to found prizes for furthering the argument; anyone proving it outright wins the jackpot.

A later proponent of the theory was A. D. (Dolly) Wraight, an English woman who published voluminously on the subject. It is supported by some members of the Marlowe Society, who in

2002 persuaded the Dean and Chapter of Westminster Abbey to install a memorial window with a question mark before the date of Marlowe's death.

IS IT TRUE?

No; and this is one of the more absurd theories. Marlowe's death in 1593 at the age of 29 is one of the best authenticated episodes in English literary history. The account of the inquest, witnessed by sixteen Londoners, survives. Various contemporaries, including Thomas Nashe, Francis Meres, Michael Drayton, George Peele, George Chapman and Henry Petowe write of him as dead after 1593. In *As You Like It*, Shakespeare himself makes Silvius quote a line from Marlowe's poem 'Hero and Leander', referring to its author as dead: 'Dead shepherd, now I find this saw of might: / Whoever loved that loved not at first sight?' Marlowe was one of the most flamboyant characters of his time, a government spy, a forger, notorious as a reputed homosexual and atheist; the idea that he went underground for at least 20 years while leaving no trace of his existence and allowing Shakespeare to take all the credit for a string of masterpieces is preposterous.

VERDICT

Nonsense

Francis Bacon wrote the plays

Who said it first?

See p. 140

Who took up the idea?

During the 1840s an American woman, Delia Bacon, gave lectures comparing Shakespeare to Bacon. She thought the plays were written by a committee including Bacon (no relative to her), Sir Walter Ralegh, and Edmund Spenser. Encouraged by the philosopher Ralph Waldo Emerson, she travelled to England in 1853 to pursue her case. In 1856 she published an article called 'William Shakespeare and his Plays: an Inquiry Concerning Them' in a New York magazine. In the same year she spent a night in Holy Trinity Church, Stratford with a lantern and tools with which she planned to open Shakespeare's grave in the hope that it held the answers to her questions. As dawn approached her courage failed her and she gave up. In the next year, subsidized anonymously by the American consul in Liverpool, the novelist Nathaniel Hawthorne, she published an unreadable book of 675 pages, *The Philosophy of Shakespeare's Plays Unfolded*. It flopped. Later that year she came to believe that she was 'the Holy Ghost and surrounded by devils'. A nephew got her back to America and she died in a lunatic asylum the following year. Nevertheless both an English Bacon Society (which still exists) and an American one were founded in the late 1880s. In *The Great Cryptogram: Francis Bacon's Cipher in the So-called Shakespeare Plays,* of 1888, an American spiritualist, Ignatius Donnelly, claimed to find clues to Bacon's authorship in a mathematical code. This was followed up by a five-volume work, *Francis Bacon's Cipher Story* (1893-5), supported by an elaborate 'decoding' machine, in which Dr Orville Ward Owen revealed that Shakespeare's works encrypt Bacon's autobiography and show that he was the son of Queen Elizabeth I by the Earl of Leicester.

IS IT TRUE?

No

THE EARL OF OXFORD WROTE THE PLAYS

WHO SAID IT FIRST?

In 1920 J. Thomas Looney, a schoolmaster, published a book called *'Shakespeare' Identified*. The first publisher to whom he submitted it had turned it down when the author refused to assume a false name. He defined a number of criteria to which the author of the plays should conform, found that Shakespeare didn't qualify, and alit upon Edward de Vere, seventeenth Earl of Oxford (1550-1604), as the true author. Like other anti-Stratfordians he was untroubled by the fact that writings by Shakespeare continued to appear until nine years after his candidate died. The theory attracted adherents (including Sigmund Freud) and was further developed in *This Star of England*, a 1,300-page book by the Americans Charles and Dorothy Ogburn, who also claimed that Oxford had been secretly married to Queen Elizabeth, and that the Earl of Southampton was their son. During the 1980s a descendant of de Vere, the Earl of Burford, continued the campaign, competing particularly with the Baconians and the Marlovians.

IS IT TRUE?

No. Oxford was a talented if minor poet, a patron of an acting company, and is said to have written comedies that have not survived. But – quite apart from the evidence that Shakespeare wrote Shakespeare – it is ridiculous to suppose that Oxford combined writing the works of Shakespeare with a busy career as a much-travelled courtier and that he left around ten masterpieces unperformed when he died, to be gradually leaked out to the King's Men to be acted and printed under a false name over the next nine years.

VERDICT

Not true

SIR HENRY NEVILLE
WROTE THE PLAYS

WHO SAYS SO?

This idea was promulgated in a book called *The Truth Will Out*, by Brenda James and William Rubinstein, published in 2005 with a foreword by the Shakespeare actor Mark Rylance, at that time Artistic Director of Shakespeare's Globe.

WHO WAS HE?

Sir Henry Neville (c. 1562 – 1615) was a minor aristocrat, an ironmaster, courtier, and Member of Parliament. In 1599 he was knighted and appointed Ambassador to France, but found the post uncongenial and returned to England, against the Queen's wishes, in 1600. He rapidly became involved in the Earl of Essex's conspiracy against the throne; when the rebellion failed he decided he could bear living in France after all, but was arrested at Dover. He was imprisoned in the Tower of London, fined the very large sum of £5000, and released when James came to the throne, in 1603. The rest of his life was spent as a politician – in 1605 alone he sat on thirty-eight parliamentary committees.

IS IT TRUE?

Well no, of course not! It is open to all the usual objections combined with the fact that his busy if not wholly successful career as a politician, spent partly abroad, would scarcely have left him the opportunity to compose the works that James and Rubinstein wish upon him.

VERDICT

Not true

LADY MARY SIDNEY WROTE THE PLAYS

WHO SAYS SO?

So far as I know this theory was first mooted in 2006 in a book called *Sweet Swan of Avon: Did a Woman write Shakespeare?* by a woman called Robin P. Williams, a prolific author of computer books, although parts of *Antony and Cleopatra* had been attributed to Lady Sidney in 1931. There is a Mary Sidney Society, 'founded on the premise that Mary Sidney Herbert, the Countess of Pembroke, wrote the works attributed to the man named William Shakespeare.' The organizers write that 'We are not only dedicated to educating the public about Mary Sidney, but our vision is to honor other unsung women, to help ensure that other women in history and today do not go unacknowledged.'

WHO WAS SHE?

Lady Mary Sidney was born in 1561 and died in 1621, so her lifetime spans Shakespeare's. Member of an aristocratic and artistic family, she was the sister of the great writer, courtier and soldier Sir Philip Sidney, who died in 1586 and who dedicated his *Arcadia* to her; she was to publish it in 1598. An immensely talented and characterful woman, she was exceptionally well educated at home, and was fluent in French, Italian and Latin, as well as being an accomplished musician and needlewoman. A devout Protestant, she may also have known Greek and Hebrew. In 1577 she married Henry Herbert, Earl of Pembroke, as his third wife, and had at least four children, including William Herbert, born in 1580, who became the third Earl of Pembroke, and Philip Herbert, later Earl of Montgomery and fourth Earl of Pembroke (see p. 60). In 1623 they were to be the dedicatees of the First Folio collection of Shakespeare's plays.

Partly to honour her brother Philip's memory, Mary became a great literary patron as well as a poet and translator in her own right. She won the admiration of many writers, including Samuel Daniel, Ben Jonson, and John Donne. Many authors dedicated works to her. Her blank verse translation of Robert Garnier's *Marc Antoine*, published in 1592, may have influenced Shakespeare's *Antony and Cleopatra*.

WHAT IS THE EVIDENCE?

Robin Williams writes, rather disingenuously, that 'This book does not attempt to prove that Mary Sidney Herbert, the Countess of Pembroke, wrote the plays and sonnets attributed to William Shakespeare. Instead, Robin Williams' intent is to provide enough documented evidence to open the inquiry into this intriguing – and entirely plausible – possibility. She accomplishes this by, on the one hand, debunking longstanding assumptions about the author of these works, and, on the other hand, providing overwhelming documented evidence connecting Mary Sidney to the Shakespearean canon.'

IS IT TRUE?

Of course not!

Roger Manners, 5th Earl of Rutland (1576 -1612), wrote the plays

Who says so?

This theory appears to have been first expounded in Germany in 1906 by Peter Alvors, and was taken up by other continental writers. A book by the American Claud W. Sykes, *Alias William Shakespeare*, published in 1947 with a foreword by the historian Arthur Bryant, and 'written in the vein of a Sherlock Holmes mystery', portrays Holmes exposing Rutland as the real author of the plays. Much more recently, in 2003, the Russian Ilya Gililov published a 400-page book, *The Shakespeare Game: The Mystery of the Great Phoenix*, described as 'an intellectual sensation that went through three printings in the first years', dedicated to the theory.

Is it true?

When I was working in Oxford during the 1980s, I had a phone call followed by a visit from an elderly Canadian gentleman who wished to show me a photograph of a portrait of the Earl of Rutland holding a copy of *Hamlet*. Intrigued, I invited him to call. He produced a copy of a genuine Elizabethan portrait of the Earl and pointed to where, he claimed, the book was shown. Nothing was there. A lengthy and embarrassed conversation ensued, in the course of which the gentleman told me of his belief not only that Rutland wrote Shakespeare, but that he himself was a reincarnation of Rutland. If this had been true, it would mean that I have shaken hands with the author of

Shakespeare's works. As the gentleman departed, escorted by his daughter, he added that he had written a musical based on his theory. To the best of my belief this has not been performed.

VERDICT

Fiction masquerading as literary detective work

HE IS AN ANCESTOR OF
PRINCES WILLIAM AND HARRY

The theory that Shakespeare had an affair with Elizabeth Vernon Countess of Southampton (*see p. 58*), and was the father of her daughter Penelope, has an interesting corollary. Penelope was an ancestress of Diana Princess of Wales; so if Hammerschmidt-Hummel is right, the Princes William and Harry are direct descendants of Shakespeare.

IS IT TRUE?

Sadly, no

A SHORT LIFE OF SHAKESPEARE

❖

The career of William Shakespeare, a glover's son born in Stratford-upon-Avon, Warwickshire, in 1564, is a remarkable example of the upward mobility that was possible in the period. His father, John Shakespeare, appears not to have been able to write but took a prominent part in the town's affairs, becoming Alderman and, in 1568, bailiff, or mayor. He figures frequently in the Town Council's minute books during the 1560s and 1570s. William's mother, born Mary Arden, lived originally in the nearby village of Wilmcote, in the farmhouse which can be visited to the present day. Like Shakespeare's Birthplace and other houses associated with the poet, it is maintained by The Shakespeare Birthplace Trust. Shakespeare would have taken his first steps in education at a petty (infant) school, where he would have learned his letters from a hornbook – a frame made of horn enclosing a paper printed with aids to learning such as the alphabet and the Lord's Prayer. But the real foundations of his success were laid at the local grammar school, the King's New School, where he received a thorough training in classical literature and rhetoric and developed a love of reading which was to sustain him in all he did and wrote. His education in Latin would perforce have originated in study from an early age of William Lyly's frequently reprinted *Short Introduction of Grammar*, first published as early as 1509 and prescribed by royal proclamation for use in all the grammar schools of the realm. Shakespeare was to portray a boy with his own name — William — being put through his paces in phrases derived from this book in Act Four, Scene One of his comedy *The Merry Wives of Windsor*, probably written in 1597. Among Shakespeare's favourite books that he would have studied at school was Ovid's *Metamorphoses*, which he was to draw on from early in his career, in *Titus Andronicus* — where he actually brings the book upon the stage — to his final solo-authored play, *The Tempest*, where one of Prospero's greatest speeches virtually paraphrases Ovid. He knew it in Arthur Golding's English translation as well as in the original Latin.

Like some other great writers of his time, such as Ben Jonson — who became immensely learned through his own efforts — Shakespeare did not proceed from grammar school to university. He married young and in a hurry. He is one of only three Stratford men between 1570 and 1630 to have married when they were under 20, and the only one of these whose bride was already pregnant. The average age for first marriage in the town at this time was 26; Shakespeare married on 27 November 1582, when he was only eighteen. The Consistory Court of the Bishopric of Worcester issued a licence permitting William Shakespeare of Stratford-upon-Avon to marry Anne Whateley — apparently a scribe's mistake for Hathaway — after only one calling of the banns, and on the next day two Stratford townsmen entered into a bond in the large sum of £40 guaranteeing that there were no legal obstacles to the marriage of William Shakespeare and Anne Hathaway. Anne, eight years his senior, was pregnant: their first daughter, Susanna, was born six months after the marriage, and twins, Judith and Hamnet, followed in 1585. How Shakespeare supported his family in their early years we do not know. At some point he joined a company of actors and embarked on a career that was to embrace acting, playwriting, the composition of non-dramatic poetry, and theatre administration.

In Shakespeare's time, as at many others, the London literary scene was rife with malice. The first reference to Shakespeare in print comes in a book named *Greene's Groatsworth of Wit Bought with a Million of Repentance* of 1592, ostensibly by Robert Greene, but possibly written in part or in whole by Henry Chettle. In it the dying playwright, poet and prose writer is portrayed as attacking Shakespeare as an 'upstart crow, beautified with our feathers' who thinks himself 'the only Shake-scene in a country.' The criticism, clearly motivated by envy, is cryptic; it may imply an accusation of plagiarism. Henry Chettle, perhaps hypocritically, leapt to Shakespeare's defence, praising his 'uprightness of dealing' as well as his 'grace in writing'. Remarkably, the attack is by far the least complimentary of all references to Shakespeare, both professionally and personally, from his lifetime. Though one or two later writers, notably Ben Jonson, expressed mixed feelings about him as an artist, none of them wrote ill of him as a man.

As Greene's allusion shows, by 1592 Shakespeare was established as a writer of plays. Closing of the London theatres in that year because of plague may have warned him of the need for an alternative career. In the following year he published the first of the two long poems by which he set forth his claim to fame as a non-dramatic poet. *Venus and Adonis*, erotically comic and based on a myth from Ovid's *Metamorphoses*, bears a dedication to Shakespeare's only known literary patron, Henry Wriothesley, third Earl of Southampton, an androgynous-looking and highly intelligent beauty some ten years younger than himself. Only a single copy of the first printing survives. A tragic counterpart, *The Rape of Lucrece*, appeared a year later with a second dedication to Southampton which suggests that the relationship had warmed into an intimacy that warranted the name of love: 'The love I dedicate to your lordship is without end …. What I have done is yours, what I have to do is yours, being part in all I have, devoted yours.'

It is probably during the 1590s that Shakespeare wrote most of the 154 sonnets which, however, were not published as a collection until 1609. In 1598 Francis Meres, in his critically naïve but historically invaluable treatise *Palladis Tamia, or Wit's Treasury*, wrote that 'the sweet witty soul of Ovid lives in mellifluous and honey-tongued Shakespeare, witness his *Venus and Adonis*, his *Lucrece*, his sugared sonnets among his private friends, etc.' Two of the poems eventually printed in the 1609 volume were included in an unauthorized collection, *The Passionate Pilgrim*, in 1599. The delay in publication is significant. The sonnets, it seems, were written not, like the narrative poems, for Shakespeare's immediate professional advancement but rather for his personal satisfaction, and for his close friends. Some of them are 'public' poems in the sense that they could have appeared without seeming out of place in poetical miscellanies of the time, but others, rebelling totally against the conventions associated with the sonnet form, are deeply, even embarrassingly, private, speaking of self-loathing, sexual revulsion, betrayal and contempt. One of their most conspicuous departures from convention lies in the fact that a number of the first 126 poems in the collection express love for a young man, not for a woman. Whether all of these poems address the same young man is one of the many questions that they provoke. It is natural to ask whether they may represent an intimate extension of the formal expression of love for Southampton declared in the dedication to *Lucrece*. The problems associated with the poems are compounded by the dedication, composed not by the author but by the publisher, Thomas Thorpe:

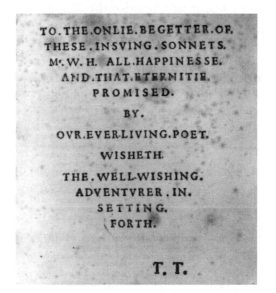

TO.THE.ONLIE.BEGETTER.OF.
THESE.INSVING.SONNETS.
Mr. W. H. ALL.HAPPINESSE.
AND.THAT.ETERNITIE.
PROMISED.

BY.

OVR.EVER-LIVING.POET.

WISHETH.

THE.WELL-WISHING.
ADVENTVRER.IN.
SETTING.
FORTH.

T. T.

What is the meaning of 'begetter'? Does it mean inspirer, or procurer (of the manuscript), or even author? Who is Mr W. H.? Why is his identity only half-revealed? Is 'W. H.' a deliberate inversion of Henry Wriothesley's initials? If so, why is an earl referred to as 'Mr' (Master' in the language of the time, and used of those holding the rank of gentleman)?

The Sonnets themselves hint at an underlying narrative that never comes to the surface. Is the poet Shakespeare himself, or Shakespeare adopting a fictional persona, or sometimes one, sometimes the other? Who is the rival poet who vies with the author for a young man's favours? And, biggest mystery of all, who is the 'black' woman (if there is only one woman) for whom the poet expresses simultaneous adoration and contempt:

> In faith, I do not love thee with mine eyes,
>   For they in thee a thousand errors note;
> But 'tis my heart that loves what they despise,
>   Who in despite of view is pleased to dote.

(Sonnet 141, ll. 1-4)

The Sonnets are at once the most revealing and the most enigmatic of Shakespeare's compositions.

During the 1590s Shakespeare must sometimes have been on tour with his fellow actors; at other times he lived in lodgings in London; he is listed as a tax defaulter in Bishopsgate ward in November 1597 and in October 1598. But he maintained close links with his home town, where his son Hamnet died and was buried in August 1596. Shakespeare's father's fortunes had declined; in 1592 he was listed among a number of Stratford residents who did not attend church regularly, some because they were secret Catholics, others, including John Shakespeare, for fear of being arrested for debt. Nevertheless, in 1596 he — or perhaps his son on his behalf — applied for, and was granted, a coat of arms. They were now officially gentlemen, with 'non sans droit' — not without right — as their family motto. In 1597

William consolidated his local status by buying the second largest house in Stratford, New Place, a grand establishment which was pulled down in the eighteenth century. On 25 October 1598 a prominent Stratfordian, Richard Quiney, wrote to him from the Bell Inn, near Saint Paul's Cathedral in London, requesting a loan of £30, probably on behalf of the townspeople. As the letter was found among Quiney's papers it seems never to have been delivered; he may have been able to speak to Shakespeare in person. No other letter either to or from Shakespeare survives. His father died in Stratford in 1601, and in the following year Shakespeare paid £320 for land in Old Stratford. The glover's son was now both a member of the gentry and a wealthy property owner.

The narrative poems were to be among Shakespeare's most popular works for half a century and more; *Venus and Adonis* was more frequently reprinted than any of his plays. They established a reputation to which an increasing number of references in both manuscript and print testify. As we have seen, Francis Meres praised them in 1598. The Muses themselves, he wrote, 'would speak with Shakespeare's fine-filed phrase if they could speak English.' In the same year Richard Barnfield published the first verse tribute to Shakespeare, again centring on his poems:

> And Shakespeare, thou whose honey-flowing vein,
> Pleasing the world, thy praises doth obtain,
> Whose *Venus* and whose *Lucrece* — sweet, and chaste —
> Thy name in Fame's immortal book have placed,
>> Live ever you, at least in Fame live ever;
>> Well may the body die, but Fame lives ever.

And 'honey' supplied a metaphor for Shakespeare's style yet again in a rather clumsily written epigram of John Weever of 1599, which describes him as 'Honey-tongued Shakespeare' and which refers to both of the narrative poems as well as to 'Romeo, Richard, more whose names I know not' and to their 'sugared tongues and power-attractive beauty.' A manuscript treatise on poetry of around 1599, written by a young student named William Scott, which came to light only in 2003 and is still unpublished, refers admiringly to both *Lucrece* and *Richard II* (while mildly criticizing a line from *Lucrece*), and quotes from both works, though without naming their author.

Shakespeare's reputation as both poet and playwright was growing. Plays were written primarily to be performed; many never got into print. Only half of Shakespeare's were published during his lifetime, and there is reason to believe that he wrote two – *Love's Labour's Won* and *Cardenio*, the latter joint-authored with John Fletcher – which have disappeared altogether. But plays by him began to appear in print in 1594, at first anonymously, but then in 1598, in the second editions of *Richard II* and *Richard III* and the first edition of *Love's Labour's Lost*, with his name on the title page. Increasingly a public figure, he nevertheless appears to have been able to sustain an enjoyable private life, if we are to believe an anecdote preserved in the diaries of John Manningham, a law student of the Middle Temple, who wrote on 13 March 1602:

> Upon a time when Richard [Burbage, the leading actor of Shakespeare's company] played Richard III there was a citizen [i. e. a citizen's wife] grew so far in liking with him that before she went from the play she appointed him to come that night unto her

by the name of Richard III. Shakespeare, overhearing their conclusion, went before, was entertained, and at his game ere Burbage
came. Then message being brought that Richard III was at the
door, Shakespeare caused return to be made that William the
Conqueror was before Richard III. *(See p. 50)*

We catch a more certainly authentic glimpse of Shakespeare the
private man in papers relating to a lawsuit of 1612 which however refer to events that took place eight years earlier, in 1604.
The suit was brought by Stephen Belott against Christopher
Mountjoy, a maker of tires, or ornamental headdresses, who
lived in Silver Street, to the north of the City. Belott, his former apprentice, had married Mountjoy's daughter Mary on 19
November 1604. Some years later Belott quarrelled with his
father-in-law, accusing him of having broken promises to pay a
marriage portion of £60 and to leave his daughter £200 in his
will. It emerges from testimony given in court that Shakespeare
had been living in the house as a lodger for some two years
before the marriage. Mountjoy had asked him to act as a go-
between in the marriage negotiations. Shakespeare spoke well of
the young man, whom he had regarded as 'a very good and
industrious servant' to whom Mountjoy had shown 'great good
will and affection.' Mrs Mountjoy had begged Shakespeare to
speak to Belott on her daughter's behalf, and Shakespeare had
done this kind office. He claimed not to know, or to remember,
much about the details of the case, but agreed that they had had
many 'conferences [conversations] about their marriage which
afterwards was consummated and solemnized.' He does not say
in what order these events occurred. Belott was awarded dam-
ages against his father-in-law, but had difficulty in getting the
money out of him.

When Queen Elizabeth I died, in March 1603, Shakespeare was named among several authors called upon to mourn her passing in Henry Chettle's *A Mournful Ditty, entitled Elizabeth's Loss*, but there is no sign that he did so. Although the theatre company to which he belonged soon came under the patronage of the new sovereign, King James I, as the King's Men, and Shakespeare's plays were frequently given at court under both Elizabeth and James, he was far less involved with royal affairs than his friend, sometime colleague and rival Ben Jonson, who wrote many court entertainments and was eventually granted a royal pension.

During the early years of the seventeenth century Shakespeare continued to add to his Stratford estates, most notably by paying the very large sum of £440 for an interest in a lease of tithes in the Stratford area in 1605. Two years later his daughter Susanna married Dr John Hall, a distinguished physician, in the town. Her father gave her 107 acres of land in the Stratford area as a wedding present. They were to have one child, Elizabeth, baptized eight months later. And Shakespeare's mother was buried there on 9 September 1609. His only major purchase of property in London came in March 1613, when he bought a gatehouse in Blackfriars, close to his company's indoor theatre; by this time he had stopped writing plays, but at the end of the month he and Richard Burbage were each paid 44 shillings for devising (Shakespeare) and painting (Burbage) an impresa – an allegorical device with a motto, painted on a paper shield carried by the Earl of Rutland in a tournament on King James's Accession Day. There is no evidence that Shakespeare ever lived in the Blackfriars house, but he became engaged in litigation concerning it in April 1615.

Back in Stratford, he had been involved in disputes concerning the enclosure of land. A disastrous fire had ravaged the town in July 1614, increasing the already severe poverty, and soon afterwards proposals were made to convert large areas of public arable land in the nearby village of Welcombe into sheep pasturage. Residents, believing that this would reduce both income and employment and increase the price of grain, were up in arms. Town records show that Shakespeare, who owned much of the land, was implicated, and he has been suspected of acting against the best interests of the poor; but his exact attitude is difficult to determine.

In January 1616, Shakespeare began to prepare for death by having a lawyer draft his will. A few weeks later his daughter Judith married a tavern keeper and wine merchant, Thomas Quiney, son of the letter-writing Richard. They had failed to obtain the special licence required for marriage in Lent, and as a result Thomas was excommunicated. Like Shakespeare before them, they had reasons to marry quickly. It emerged that the husband had begotten a child on one Margaret Wheeler who died and was buried with the baby on 15 March. Quiney was sentenced to perform public penance. Discovery of the affair appears to have caused Shakespeare to change his will. The first sheet, which mostly concerns Judith, has been recopied, apparently because Shakespeare, mistrusting her husband, made changes to protect Judith's interests. In the final draft, dated 25 March, she receives £100 as a marriage portion, and the interest on a further £150 for as long as she was married; but her husband could claim the interest only if he settled lands of equal value on her. She was also to inherit her father's silver-gilt bowl. This may survive, but has not been identified. There are personal bequests, including his sword to his friend Thomas Combe and twenty shillings in gold to his seven-year old godson William Walker, but the bulk of the estate goes to his eldest daughter, Susanna. His granddaughter Elizabeth Hall received all his plate except for the silver-gilt bowl. With her death, childless, in 1670 Shakespeare's direct line died out.

Notoriously, his wife receives only the second-best bed, and even that is an afterthought. But she may have been automatically entitled to a share of the estate, and she continued to live in New Place till she died, in 1623. Shakespeare himself died on 23 April 1616, and is buried in the chancel of Holy Trinity Church. The stone which is reputedly his grave (not a tomb, as is often said) bears the epitaph:

> Good friend, for Jesus' sake forbear
> To dig the dust enclosèd here.
> Blessed be the man that spares these stones,
> And cursed be he that moves my bones.

Essentially this is a plea that the sexton should not throw his bones into the charnel house neighbouring the church, as was often done. Close to the grave is the monument bearing the bust executed by the Dutch craftsman Gerard Johnson (or Gheerart Janssen) and adorned with inscriptions in both English and Latin comparing the former Stratford schoolboy with great figures of classical antiquity, and praising his genius. The Latin one, when translated, reads: 'In judgement a Nestor, in genius a Socrates, in art a Virgil.' The English one is:

Stay, passenger, why goest thou by so fast?
Read, if thou canst, whom envious death hath placed
Within this monument: Shakespeare, with whom
Quick nature died; whose name doth deck this tomb,
Far more than cost, sith all that he hath writ
Leaves living art but page to serve his wit.

Among Shakespeare's lesser bequests are sums of 26s 8d to buy mourning rings for his colleagues Richard Burbage, John Heminges and Henry Condell. These were his lifelong colleagues. Burbage died in 1619, but Heminges and Condell undertook responsibility for the assembling and publication of Shakespeare's collected plays in the First Folio, of 1623. Conceivably they had discussed this with Shakespeare before he died. In doing so they produced Shakespeare's greatest monument: without it we should have lacked half of his plays, including some of the greatest.

The legacy that Shakespeare left is incalculable. In particular the English language and all the arts of many countries – the theatre, film, ballet, painting, drama, the novel, poetry, biography, orchestral music, song, opera – would have been immeasurably poorer without the influence that his writings have posthumously exerted. He is the greatest figure of world literature, not simply the greatest of playwrights but a poet, thinker and philosopher with unparalleled understanding of the human psyche who used the drama as his vehicle. No one has bettered Ben Jonson's prescient epitaph: 'He was not of an age, but for all time.'

FURTHER READING

BIOGRAPHIES

In my opinion the best, certainly the wittiest, biography remains S. Schoenbaum's *Compact Documentary Life* (Oxford, 1977, reprinted 1987). Park Honan's *Shakespeare: A Life* (Oxford 1998) is a little more up-to-date, reliable and readable. Other worthwhile studies are Peter Thomson's *Shakespeare's Professional Career* (Cambridge University Press, 1992), Katherine Duncan-Jones's adversarial *Ungentle Shakespeare* (Arden Shakespeare, 2001), Michael Wood's *In Search of Shakespeare* (BBC, 2003 the book of his television series), and Stephen Greenblatt's *Will in the World* (Jonathan Cape, 2004). James Shapiro's *1599: A Year in the Life of William Shakespeare* (Faber, 2005) is a fascinating key-hole study.

REFERENCE BOOKS

A comprehensive and readable guide is *The Oxford Companion to Shakespeare*, ed. Michael Dobson and Stanley Wells (Oxford, 2001). More compact is my *Oxford Dictionary of Shakespeare* (Oxford University Press, revised edition, 2005). J. C. Trewin's *Pocket Companion to Shakespeare's Plays* (Mitchell and Beazley, revised edition 2005) is a handy guide.

The Works

Quotations in this volume are from The Complete Works, General Editors Stanley Wells and Gary Taylor (Oxford University Press, 1986; 2nd edition, 2005). This volume includes a helpful introduction to Shakespeare's language by David Crystal. Among many available editions of single works, the Penguin is the most accessible for the general reader. More detailed annotation is provided by the Oxford, New Cambridge, and Arden series (some of the last-named are badly out-of-date). There are excellent editions of the poems (including the sonnets) by Colin Burrow (Oxford University Press, 2002) and John Kerrigan (sonnets and 'A Lover's Complaint', Penguin, 1986). A useful guide to the sonnets and all the problems they pose is *Shakespeare's Sonnets*, by Paul Edmondson and Stanley Wells (Oxford University Press, 2004)

General Books

Jonathan Bate's *The Genius of Shakespeare* (Picador, 1988) offers a stimulating appreciation. My fully illustrated *Shakespeare: For All Time* (Macmillan, 2002) has two biographical chapters, an account of how Shakespeare wrote, and a survey of his influence over the centuries.

NOTES

p. 30, '…should have published it': S. Schoenbaum, *Shakespeare's Lives* (Oxford, 1988, revised 1991), p. 529

p. 34, 'acknowledge their sin in church': E. R. C. Brinkworth, *Shakespeare and the Bawdy Court of Stratford* (1972), p. 87

p. 35, '…a true report': S. Schoenbaum, *Shakespeare's Lives*, p. 346

p. 66, '…sources in Italian': Naseeb Shaheen, 'Shakespeare's Knowledge of Italian', *Shakespeare Survey* 47 (Cambridge University Press, 1994), p. 169

p. 86, '…which killed him': *Shakespeare: Man and Artist*, 2 vols, (Oxford University Press, 1938), Vol. 2, p. 824

p. 126, '…remained in the language': David Crystal, 'The Language of Shakespeare', in the second edition (2005) of the Oxford Complete Works

p. 128, '…end to human foolery': S. Schoenbaum, *Shakespeare's Lives*, p. 565

p. 138, '…common to her rhythmic race': Schoenbaum, *Shakespeare's Lives*, p. 497

p. 138, '…Scandal of Shakespeare's Sonnets': *Shakespeare Survey* 46 (Cambridge, 1993)

p. 160, 'when he was only eighteen': Jeanne Jones, *Family Life in Shakespeare's England: Stratford-upon-Avon 1570–1630* (Stratford-upon-Avon, 1996), p. 90

Recent books by Stanley Wells

Shakespeare: For All Time
(Macmillan, 2002 and OUP New York, 2003)

'Here is a man who has a fair claim to be the most complete Shakespearian of them all...Now he has distilled a lifetime's work into one crisply written, richly illustrated and entertaining book.' *The Sunday Times*

'Scholarly, urbane, rich in anecdotes and marvellously readable, it is a meticulously constructed and authoritative survey with a vast and satisfying scope.' *New Statesman*

'This copiously illustrated album admirably compresses more than four centuries of the bard and more than 50 years of Wells's devotion to him.' *Publishers Weekly*

'One of those heavy, beautifully produced books which is a pleasure to look at as it is to read... There's no doubting the scholarship here' *Time Out London*

Shakespeare & Co.
(Penguin, 2006; Pantheon, USA, 2007)

'A superbly enjoyable and, indeed, inspiring piece of work' *Bill Bryson*

'an enthralling work of popular scholarship' *The Observer*

'One of the most sane and exciting books on Shakespeare I have read for a long time' *Scotland on Sunday*

'Deliciously dry he may sometimes be, but there is nothing academic about Wells's approach to his subject. The book is easy, gossipy, and even racy in tone as the good doctor doles out succulent bonbons of anecdote and significant fact from the vast larder of his knowledge.' *Simon Callow, The Guardian*